Intertextuality and Victorian Studies

Intertextuality and Victorian Studies

Sudha Shastri

Orient Longman

To my mother and
my father

ORIENT LONGMAN LIMITED

Registered Office
3-6-272 Himayatnagar, Hyderabad 500 029 (A.P.), India

Other Offices
Bangalore / Bhopal / Bhubaneshwar / Chandigarh / Chennai
Ernakulam / Guwahati / Hyderabad / Jaipur / Kolkata
Lucknow / Mumbai / New Delhi / Patna

ISBN 81 250 2088 8

Typeset by
OSDATA, Hyderabad 500 029

Printed in India at
Orion Printers
Hyderabad 500 004

Published by
Orient Longman Limited
3-6-272 Himayatnagar
Hyderabad 500 029 (A.P.), India

Acknowledgements

I express my gratitude to Professor Rukmini Bhaya Nair, my research supervisor, who played a guiding role in the earlier version of this work, for which I received my doctoral degree.

I am also grateful to Professor Alok Rai for his encouragement and support, and to Professor Susie Tharu for her suggestions.

It gives me great pleasure to acknowledge the advice and encouragement of A. S. Byatt.

My special thanks to Professor Ashok Misra, Director of I.I.T. Bombay, Professor S. P. Sukhatme, Director of I.I.T. Bombay when I joined the institute and Professor Amitabha Gupta, Head, Department of Humanities and Social Sciences, I.I.T. Bombay for having made it possible for me to publish this book.

For the moral support and strength they have given me, I wish to thank my friends Nilie, Kajal, Nishi, Puja, Sonu, Tanushree and Nimmi. But for Vivekanand's timely help with my diskette, it would have taken this book much longer to see the light of day.

Abbreviations

The following works have been cited in this book with the abbreviations indicated, except where they first occur:

ED	*The Mystery of Edwin Drood* (London: Penguin Books, 1993)
FLW	*The French Lieutenant's Woman* (London: Pan Books, 1987)
GFL	*The Great Fire of London* (London: Pan Books, 1993)
WSS	*Wide Sargasso Sea* (Harmondsworth: Penguin Books, 1983)

Contents

Introduction

The novels that form the focus of this study are in themselves formidable studies of the Victorian period. They are self-consciously post-Saussurean[1] in their foregrounding of textuality, which, briefly, is the awareness of a work as a linguistic construct, based on the prior and arbitrary sign-system of language. Hence, despite their setting in and/or repeated references to the Victorian period (1830–90), they caution the reader against classifying them as straightforward 'period' novels.

These different novels include Peter Ackroyd's *The Great Fire of London (GFL)* (1982), A.S. Byatt's *Angels and Insects* (1992) and *Possession: A Romance* (1990), John Fowles's *The French Lieutenant's Woman (FLW)* (1969), Lin Haire-Sergeant's *Heathcliff: The Sequel to Wuthering Heights* (1992), Jean Rhys's *Wide Sargasso Sea (WSS)* (1966), and Emma Tennant's *Tess* (1993). In the interests of coherence, the argument of this book rests primarily on the following novels: *Possession*, *FLW*, *WSS* and *Tess*.

Of this list, a novel such as *FLW* is a classic example of a self-conscious narrative that problematises the notion of a unified text, by using all aspects of Victorian life as its *ur*-text[2]: literary, social, cultural and scientific. There can be little doubt that this kind of novel is very likely to reward critical attention, in its representation of the nineteenth and twentieth centuries through textual modes ranging from the epigraph to the journal. Given *ur*- or parent texts like Fowles's, this research into intertextuality needs to address the issue of Victorian studies, rather than the Victorian novel or even Victorian literature.

Intertextuality and the Victorian Period

The term 'Victorianist' is used here to designate the twentieth-century novels of this study, in order to distinguish them from the Victorian novels which form the master-texts for these novels[3]. Upto a point, 'Victorianist' is analogous to Edward Said's use of the term 'Orientalist', but the pejorative burden that Said's term carries, of a 'biased specialist', is absent in this case. Like the Orientalist, the Victorianist studies

Victoriana with authority despite, or perhaps because of being an outsider.

The idea that the 'other' – be it the Victorian or the Orient – needs to be represented, is the result of a claim to privileged knowledge; which encourages Fowles, for instance, to announce that he is writing the Victorian novel that the Victorians could not, themselves, have written. Unlike the Orient, however, the Victorian 'other' is occasioned not by a difference in race/gender/culture as much as in time. Prejudices inherent in a Victorianist interpretation are likely to be much less, since the ideological implications of a temporal difference are far more limited than the implications of the other counters I have specified. Perhaps no representation is totally innocent, but by providing the reader with a niche in the interpretive procedures, Victorian intertextuality, unlike Orientalism, appropriates less than total authority in representing the Victorians.

Considering that it lies outside the pale of the historical novel, Victorianist fiction is admittedly a sophisticated enterprise. A historical novel such as Walter Scott's *Ivanhoe* (1819), for example, aims at keeping the past remote and at preserving its exotic distance from the present. One of the assumptions on which this aim rests is that the past portrayed in the novel is a 'real' past, as it were, which the reader is beguiled into accepting as literal. In other words, the reader is expected to look through the aspect of representation and overlook the artifice of portrayal. But when the Victorianist novel refers to the past, it is conscious of its vantagepoint in the present, and ensures that its reader, too, is conscious of the simultaneity of two worlds, the world represented by the text and the world within which he is positioned as a reader.

It is the concept of 'text' that marks the quintessential distinction between the historical and the intertextual novel. A historical novel simulates the *world* of the past, while an intertextual novel concentrates on the representational processes that go into the making of this world. Textuality may be posited as the awareness that one is engaging with a sign-system, and the author as well as the reader(s) generally share in this knowledge; if the writer, for whatever reason, decides to disguise this fact from the reader, the intertextual identity of the text suffers. Self-consciousness of the text is an indispensable component of textuality. That is, for a text to become intertextual, it is first necessary for the text to be perceived by the reader as self-conscious/self-reflexive. The emphasis of the text has to be directed towards presenting itself as a construct of words – some denotative and some connotative – instead of presenting itself as a substitute for the real world.

Intertextuality and its Significance

The aims of this study of intertextuality are:

a) to categorise the various types of intertextuality in some Victorianist novels, and to arrive at a clear distinctive theoretical framework for the study of this process. An analysis of Victorianist novels in relation to intertextuality is expected to be productive, since intertextual concepts become contextually focussed in such an analysis. Diffuseness, a common pitfall in the elaboration of a theory, is avoided, with the Victorianist novel working as a testing-ground for hypotheses about intertextual definition. A prevalent tendency to use intertextuality loosely, as though it were another manifestation of 'influence' or allusion, needs a corrective. This study will use the inter-connectedness of Victorianism and intertextuality to study both in detail. The mutual support that Victorianism and intertextuality provide needs to be explored as a preliminary step towards understanding their dynamics, individually as well as together.

b) to raise the question of intertextuality being natural to some genres (like the novel) and not to some others (like lyric poetry).

c) to explore the relationship between intertextual and mimetic theories of art: whether they correspond, or whether they are polar oppositions.

d) to study the current novelistic trend of invoking the Victorians: although the creative intertextual process does not restrict itself to the Victorians, the presence of a considerable number of Victorianist novels definitely indicates scope for research.

Principles of Intertextuality

A text is a system of signs, which are not merely verbal or linguistic. The intertextual novels of this study expand the notion of 'text' imaginatively, even under this rubric of 'the sign-system'. Jean Rhys's *Wide Sargasso Sea* (hereafter referred to as *WSS*), is intertextually inspired by a single Victorian novel, Charlotte Brontë's *Jane Eyre* (1847), and structured in such a way as to make knowledge of the earlier novel mandatory, if *WSS* is to be completely understood. Frequently, this understanding requires a reading between the lines, which results in an altered assessment of the earlier novel. To cite an instance, the attack of mad Bertha on Rochester and Richard, presented judgmentally by Brontë, is retold with great sympathy by Rhys, enabling the reader to recognise that Brontë does less than justice to the mentally unsound and racially marginalised character of Bertha.

With Byatt's *Possession* and Tennant's *Tess*, the notion of a text is extended to include genre. Tennant evokes the genre of the ballad inside the contours of her novel, by repeatedly referring to her narrative as 'the ballad of love, betrayal, murder' (*Tess*, 117, 149,163). Byatt goes a step further by evoking at least two genres, the romance and the dramatic monologue.

In a third and more complex case, the boundaries of 'text' become hazy as they lose their clarity of outline in a medley of cultural and social practices. The novel is *French Lieutenant's Woman* (hereafter referred to as *FLW*). One of the ways in which Fowles captures the Victorian *zeitgeist* is through descriptions of place. His narrative is set in Lyme Regis, which was the seat of ancient fossils, and which attracted not a little attention in the post-Lyell and post-Darwin years[4]. His choice of locale indicates the importance of the Victorian spirit to a complete understanding of *FLW*.

The three examples cited above are preliminaries to the following questions, which the notion of intertextuality seems to summon up, without necessarily answering:

a) If everything, including phenomenological reality like place, which is transcribed as sign, becomes a text, then does this not imply that an intertextual work is self-contained? Can there be anything 'inter'-referential about the procedure, if everything is textual?
b) How far does the intertextual status of a novel depend upon the reader?

This brings us to a related issue – representation. One way of trying to grasp intertextuality is by positing that much of our apprehension of reality is shaped through texts. Hence representation in an intertextual novel has to be self-conscious. *FLW* is flamboyantly metafictional, and carries its consciousness of a fictional status effortlessly through; it is simultaneously no less aware of its spurious Victorian identity which it strives to sustain, even while drawing its reader's attention to the strings activating its Victorian puppet-show.

While the answer to a) appears to be a self-evident affirmative, what redeems intertextuality from the trap of a circular argument is the principle it is based on: 'difference'. Differentiality, by definition, opposes the notion of self-containedness. 'The concept of intertextuality requires that we understand the concept of text not as a self-contained structure but as differential and historical...Texts are therefore not structures of presence but traces and tracings of otherness' (Frow 45). Intertextual procedures require the reader to look for division and discontinuity within a given text. The most common method of presenting intertextuality is through juxtapositioning various texts, and visually reinforcing the impression of textual fissure[5]. A dynamic process, intertextuality preserves a text from closure, and therefore depends upon incompleteness for its survival.

FLW has literally only two endings, but by having just one more than the standard unitary ending, the text creates an image of several more possible endings, and impresses its open-endedness indelibly upon its reader's imaginative grasp of the novel. Incompleteness suggests that textual autonomy is relative, not absolute, and that all texts require to be complemented by other texts to which they are related.

Question b) implies two axes of intertextuality: texts entering a given text via authors, and via readers. For the complete success of an intertextual work, it is necessary that the author and the reader trust each other over the textual connections they must make in order to make intertextuality a fulfilling experience.

A further implication is the theoretical affinity between intertextuality and différance, whereby the text eludes one ultimate meaning by opening up an endless play of signifiers. This results in more than one interpretation. Interpretations can vary, can even be at odds with each other, and affect the intertextual novel on the bases of the knowledge that readers bring to the interpretive process. 'Because the fictional text is directed at the imagination of the reader, there will always be variables in the interpretation possible in the imaginative spaces of the text' (Scholes et al. 166). Opinions however differ sharply in this respect. 'There is no reader outside the text by which the meaning can be said to enter the text', avers Silvermann (79).

Some Theories of Intertextuality

As a critical term, intertextuality is generally dated from Julia Kristeva's use of it in 'Word, Dialogue, and Novel'. Published in 1966, the above essay is primarily a recapitulation of Bakhtin's concept of the dialogic nature of the novel, and thereby, itself an illustration of intertextuality. According to her, writing is an act that presupposes a split between subject and object, a 'doubling'. Therefore the intertextual feature of dialogism is inherent in the most minimal linguistic unit, the word. 'By introducing the status of the word as a minimal structural unit, Bakhtin situates the text within history and society, which are then seen as texts read by the writer, and into which he inserts himself by rewriting them' (Kristeva 65).

The difficulty posed by Kristeva's theory is this: her definition renders all writing intertextual, thus taking us backwards to the problem we just encountered. Of course, Kristeva does preserve a broad distinction between poetic and non-poetic language; but by assigning intertextual status to the novel-genre without question, she invalidates the idea of an especially intertextual novel. If 'any text is constructed as a mosaic of quotations' and 'any text is the absorption and transformation of another' (Kristeva 66), then one is faced with the danger of the intertextual novel being a redundancy.

A way of getting round this problem is by looking at the intertextual novel as a specialised genre, an ideal condition to which all novels aspire, but only a few reach. From this point of view, the deliberately intertextual novel is the most sophisticated example of the genre. From another perspective, the literarily intertextual novel is also an attempt to integrate the novel into literary tradition, by referring to other, usually canonical texts, and thereby discountenancing the long and deeply entrenched belief that the novel is a bourgeois form.

This moves intertextuality to the realm of critical theory, and should concurrently alert us to the recognition that intertextuality has had a latent existence in critical thinking about literature for a long time. The example which comes most readily to mind is Aristotle's description of 'mimesis', which can be completely understood only in terms of the earlier, disparaging manner in which Plato employed the term. Aristotle was not simply using the term for descriptive purposes, but attempting to purge it of its pejorative baggage and reinstate it (Plato 344–62, Aristotle 31–45).

Intertextuality therefore, is not a mere cross-referencing or interdependence of texts; it also includes the attitude that one text exhibits towards another. Since intertextuality commonly works chronologically, attitudes are displayed by the text(s) placed later to the text(s) placed earlier in time. Sometimes attitudes of a certain type get crystallised into genres, such as parody, which is the 'imitative use of the words, style, *attitude,* tone and ideas of an author in such a way as to make them ridiculous' (Cuddon 483, emphasis mine). It is relevant to recall at this juncture that the novel also has a parodic tradition behind it, boasting such stalwart practitioners as Cervantes and Fielding.

Intertextuality has tended to let itself be subsumed by various names such as source-studies, allusion, reference, influence, parody, pastiche and quotation. As this plethora of near-synonyms suggests, descriptions of intertextuality desiderate a critical vigour in definition. But here, we shall endeavour to establish that it is not simply an umbrella term, a sum total of the various devices it employs, but an activity that foregrounds the boundaries as well as the boundary-crossings between texts.

But what are 'texts'? When Michael Riffaterre distinguishes 'uniqueness' as the textual touchstone[6], he seems to beg the question, and it becomes necessary to look elsewhere for what constitutes textuality. Riffaterre does furnish a vivid description of textuality in his essay, 'Mimesis as Interpretive Discourse', where he perceives intertextuality as dependent upon a type of mimesis in which reference is made not so much to exterior reality as to its representations (Riffaterre

159), thus allying the activity with meta-level proceedings. The problem of representation has a chequered past, beginning with Plato's contentious claim that it deals with appearance, and not the truth, and that 'a representer knows nothing of value about the things he represents' (Riffaterre, 'The Intertextual Unconscious' 348–54). Victorianist novels like *Possession* and *FLW* examine the question of representation anew, for which reason they ruthlessly remove the cumbersome camouflage of the façade of realism from their novels. In this they seem to follow the line of Plato's argument that 'representation is a kind of game, and shouldn't be taken seriously' (Riffaterre, 'The Intertextual Unconscious' 354); but their methods of parading this affirm the amazing and brilliant vitality of this game.

Roland Barthes's essay, 'From Work to Text', is much more illuminating than Riffaterre's. Barthes proposes a series of differences between what constitutes a 'work' and what, a 'text'. The text lies within the work, as 'a methodological field' (Barthes 74). It is pertinent to raise the related term, 'discourse', at this juncture, which functions somewhat in competition to 'text', since they are sometimes used interchangeably. In the words of Drakakis, 'discourse' refers to the field which makes the text operative; discourse, thereby, 'operates at the level of the enablement of texts' (Drakakis, in Clayton and Rothstein 196–97). 'Discourse' occupies a larger semantic field than the more streamlined term, 'text'. Like 'work', 'discourse' is 'experienced only in activity, a production' (Barthes, 'From Work to Text' 75). The text challenges conventional ways of classification, since it is concerned with limits and demarcations. It is also irreducibly plural, requiring active collaboration from the reader before its effect of pleasure or *jouissance* can be realised.

One of the primary distinguishing marks of the text is its encoded status. The text, whatever its genre or length, is an entity which exists at the level of the sign; more precisely, the signifier. By implication therefore, the text recognises a boundary between the sphere of words, and the sphere of the world that the words try to reach. 'Whereas the text is approached and experienced in relation to the sign, the work closes itself on a signified' (Barthes, 'From Work to Text' 75). The text is concerned with limits, borders and margins. The work exists at one remove from the signifier, and its linguistic and literary counters have to be seen by the reader in relation to the empirical reality that it points to. On the other hand, the text exists at the level of the signifier, the words themselves, without needing a signified beyond itself to justify its being.

This notion is supported by Thais Morgan in her essay 'The Space of Intertextuality': 'As a structural analysis of texts in relation to the larger system of signifying practices or uses of signs in culture, intertextuality seems by definition to deliver us from old controversies over the psychology of individual authors and readers, the tracing of literary origins, and the relative value of imitation or originality' (O'Donnell and Con Davis 239). As she remarks with an intuitive perception, every text has another subterranean text behind it which is its 'ghost text' (265). One of the implications of this statement is that intertextuality is not to be confused with the kind of source-hunting and catalogue-criticism practised, for instance, by John Livingston Lowes in *The Road to Xanadu* (1927). Intertextuality comes as an answer to the 'anxiety of originality' (Scholes et al. 129), and a significant aspect of its solution is its emphasis on self-consciousness.

Indeed self-awareness is a precondition of textuality, if a text has to hold the reader's imagination at the level of the signifier, and arrest a leap to the signified external reality. The text is compelled to exert all its resources in reminding the reader that it is an artefact. Barthes in fact delves further into the matter to distinguish between 'writerly' and 'readerly' texts. A readerly text requires to be read 'in an everyday, conventional, sequential, and essentially syntagmatic fashion', while the former kind is a text 'rewritten in a semiological reading of it' (quoted in Silvermann 76).

At first glance, Bloom's theory of influence as stated in *The Anxiety of Influence* appears to be a mere terminological variation of intertextuality, especially his proposition that reading is a necessary component of text-production, which makes 'misreading' an active and dynamic process.

However, influence as propounded by Bloom diverges markedly from intertextuality in certain ways that make the distinction difficult to erase. Bloom, for example, emphasises a line of continuity between individual poets rather than texts. He qualifies these poets as 'strong', whose relationship to their successor-poets is characterised by hostility. Intertextuality on the other hand, encompasses a larger field of interplay, where complicity and affinity between texts is as much a feature as mutual animosity.

Key Concepts

Intertextual activities proceed on the basis of certain assumptions, the critical vocabulary for which best derives from the concept of relevance, presented by Sperber and Wilson in *Relevance: Communication and Cognition* (1986). Among other terms, troping is one of the concepts that Sperber and Wilson expound at length. Tropes[7] demonstrate the inherent intertextual characteristic of deictic 'otherness'[8]. Intertextuality itself could be perceived as a super- or master- trope containing a number of sub-tropes such as quotations and allusions.

Take for instance the name of the twentieth-century heroine of *Possession*, which is 'Maud'. Her name functions as a trope by recalling Tennyson's monodrama, *Maud*, and to stress this textual loyalty, Byatt quotes from Tennyson's poem. In her capacity as omniscient narrator, Byatt points out that erudite male admirers of Maud invariably recall Tennyson's description of his heroine as 'icily regular, splendidly null' (*Possession* 316, 506), when they come face to face with Maud. Here is a counter-intuitive illustration of a book dictating responses in the real world[9]. The chapter, 'Intertextual Devices' elucidates the intertextual impact of names like Maud and Christabel. Often the tropes in these quasi-Victorian novels turn out to be epigraphs which are twice-tropic, working at the level of both content and form in the following way. By employing a direct quotation from a Victorian writer as epigraph, these novels establish themselves in the Victorian ethos; and by using the epigraph as a formal device, they invite the reader to acknowledge a significant convention of the Victorian novel.

Sperber and Wilson raise the issue of optimal relevance in communication, a topic of particular importance in intertextuality: 'A speaker aiming at optimal relevance will leave implicit everything her hearer can be trusted to supply with less effort than would be needed to process an explicit prompt' (Sperber and Wilson 218). The writer-reader relationship is dependent on the latter's capacity to understand, and *not misunderstand*, the writer. The challenge to this relationship lies in the extent of information and knowledge the reader can be allowed to infer implicitly. A delicate balance needs to be struck, to preempt the risk of the reader surrendering intelligibility. Intertextual novels are poised on the fine tightrope between the scylla of excessive information, and the charybdis of incomprehension. Emma Tennant does this feat quite creditably in *Tess*, where she uses Hardy's title for her novel, and then ensures that her intent is conveyed, by referring periodically to the connotations of Hardy's eponymous narrative as a tale of purity, rape and suffering.

A related notion put forth by Sperber and Wilson in the matter of optimal relevance is that of cognitive effort. Tropes such as stereotypes do lessen the extent of cognitive effort otherwise required by both writer and reader to arrive at inferences. Byatt's use of the dramatic monologue as a literary stereotype in *Possession* enables her to convey (and the reader to apprehend) the connections involved therein i.e. dramatic monologue = Robert Browning = Randolph Henry Ash. This happens despite the fact that Byatt studiously avoids any mention of Browning in the novel. This is only one of the equations that are ready-made.

Intertextual activities function, in effect, as echoic utterances:

> From the pragmatic point of view, what is important is that a speaker can use an echoic utterance to convey a whole range of attitudes and emotions, ranging from outright acceptance and approval to outright rejection and disapproval, and that the recognition of these attitudes and emotions may be crucial to the interpretation process.
>
> (Sperber and Wilson 240)

An echoic utterance implies, first, that intertextual novels are historically determined; even if Tennant called her novel *Tess* but did not intend to evoke Hardy in her novel, the connection is already present by the simple fact of Hardy's novel ante-dating hers. Echoic utterances also imply the existence of an attitude, which is an integral feature of intertextuality. Neither neutral re-presentations nor source-studies, intertextual re-workings exhibit an opinion towards their parent-texts. It is to this opinion that the reader's attention is drawn. This feature is particularly visible in novels like *Tess* and *WSS*, which exhibit an attitude of irreconciliation with their parent texts, as shall be elucidated in subsequent chapters.

Therefore, is intertextuality a form of parody? Comparing intertextuality with parody is an illuminating process, since it brings to light a pre-requisite for both intertextuality and parody (although Margaret Rose disagrees): that at least two texts require to be read before intertextuality can come into existence. The all-important component of attitude that Sperber and Wilson emphasise forms the basis of both intertextual and parodic relationships. Both proceedings cause changes in the *ur*-text, since the new text invariably revises received ways of reading the older one. There is however a marked difference, caused by the presence of what Margaret Rose, in her exhaustive study of the parodic tradition, calls 'comic discrepancy' (Rose 37). As a result, a possible answer to the question raised above is that parody is subsumed in the enveloping compass of intertextuality. Intertextual modes are comic, and more.

Semantically contiguous terms like 'travesty' and 'burlesque' can cause confusion in the understanding of parody. Intertextuality escapes this danger by virtue of its assimilating capacity, which empowers it to encompass these types, often turning them into devices that further its own intention. 'Pastiche',[10] like the quotation or the epigraph, is also an intertextual device. 'Plagiarism' appears to complicate the issue, but there is a cardinal difference between it and intertextuality, which is characterised by honesty and literary integrity. Plagiarism is usually 'concerned to conceal or destroy its sources' (Rose 69), and intertextuality to reveal these, towards a particular end.

Parody facilitates a proper understanding of intertextuality as an imaginative act of writing and not as something blind or derivative, because of the attitude factor. Parody is guided by an attitude usually of disrespect, amounting to mockery, of its generator-text. Intertextuality enlarges the range of attitude and imaginatively explores different possibilities including approval, scepticism, affirmation and questioning. Intertextual novels such as *Tess* and *Wide Sargasso Sea (WSS)* for instance, can and do destabilise and disturb.

There is no doubt that the novel is an excellent form for the diverse manifestations of intertextuality. As O'Donnell remarks, 'Narrative offers a particularly fruitful area for this discussion because its generic and discursive largesse allows for a rich mixing of texts, histories, stories, and voices where the work of intertextuality is often at its most fervent' (O'Donnell xiv).

Although listed last in this series, the stereotype is the most predominant of tropes employed by these novels[11]. Stereotypes may be non-literary, and one such as the Sexually Repressed Victorian Woman is an economical way of communicating a complex of information. Sarah would be a classic case of a Fallen Woman, much like Tess, although Tess's falling, unlike Sarah's, is none of her choosing. Byatt also literally puts a stereotype within quote-marks in her narrative in the description of Roland's reaction to Christabel LaMotte's picture. 'Generic Victorian Lady, specific shy poetess', is how Roland mentally classifies her (*Possession* 38).

Stereotypes function as shorthand, but in order to use them effectively, there has to be a degree and some certainty of shared knowledge between writer and reader. In a non-intertextual novel, the author's concern is merely to ensure that readers understand the linguistic and semantic denotations of the words used. But in an intertextual novel, the common fund needs to be supplied by textual and literary background knowledge as well.

Mimesis and Intertextuality

We drank deep of the Fountain of Vaucluse
And where the northern Force incessantly
'Stirs the still pool, were stirred. *And shall those founts*
Which freely flowed to meet our thirsts, be sealed?'

(*Ask to Embla* by R. H. Ash)

'Ah, Melusine, I have betrayed your faith.
Is there no remedy? Must we two part?
Shall our hearth's ash grow pale, *and shall those founts*
Which freely flowed to meet our thirsts, be sealed?'

(*Melusina* by C. LaMotte)
(*Possession* 237, emphasis mine)

Roland and Maud quote the above texts respectively, in chapter twelve of *Possession*. Engaged in their quest for truth, these two scholars make the above connection, with mounting excitement, of cross-textual references between Ash's and LaMotte's poetry. What they discover, almost incredibly, is that the two poets have used the very same sentence, and the question of who influenced whom becomes difficult to answer, despite the fact that the poems are chronologically fixed. This is because the line derives from a shared experience of Ash and Christabel. A note of intrigue that further compounds their wonder, is the absence of any record thus far (later on, Roland and Maud uncover the secret romance of Ash and Christabel) to the effect that the two poets even knew each other.

This passage from *Possession* expertly captures the intertextual paradigm, simultaneously showing the reader how to proceed in the attempt to interpret an intertextual act. As an illustration, this is an ideal springboard to raise the role of originality in literature, which is commonly placed in antithesis to derived texts that intertextuality certainly seems to license. The age-old criterion of mimesis[12] as the measure of all literature is also questioned by intertextuality, if not overtly, in an implicit fashion.

Mimesis or representation has been perceived as the cornerstone of all literary activity from Plato onwards, who used this as a reason to give a derogatory cast to literature. According to him, artistic representation was twice removed from the world of ideals, which was also the realm of truth (Plato 348). It was left to his student Aristotle to resuscitate the dying value of literature and give it a pre-eminent position. Aristotle accepted Plato's notion and definition of mimesis, but his own *attitude* to mimesis was antithetically opposed to Plato's, and he worked on the concept with a view towards reinstating it. Thus we have a very early case of intertextuality in practice, where Aristotle revoked an idea used before him in Plato's text *Republic*, to re-define it favourably; and produce, in short, an echoic utterance with an attitudinal change. In stating that poetry (a term used interchangeably with 'literature' by him and Plato) is concerned with the representation of 'universal truths' according to 'the laws of possibility and probability' (Aristotle 44), he salvaged the notion of representation from general contempt and denigration. Aristotle had found a way around Plato's argument by advocating a poetic truth, which consists of probabilities and universals.

What is the relationship that intertextuality shares with the stipulations of mimesis in literature? Mimesis refers to the representation through imitation, of the world of phenomenological reality, within the covers of a book. At its most basic level, intertextuality deals with texts; while it is true that it also deals with the phenomenological world(s) depicted in these texts, intertextuality has *also* 'already' internalised the reality within these texts and arrived at a self-conscious plane of dealing with it. Intertextuality categorically rejects the realistic mode of representation by a) owing and acknowledging its inspiration to other texts rather than real life, and b) insistently pointing out the textual character of its representational devices.

From the point of view of the mimetic position, it becomes necessary to debate whether intertextuality, which imitates previous texts rather than the 'real' world, is a theoretical replacement to mimesis, or a modified version of it. It is appropriate to recall Renate Lachmann's query at this juncture: 'Has the concept mainly a literary critical function in that it can put into question existing concepts of literature such as uniqueness, isolation, structural totality and "system likeness" ' (quoted in Rose 181). An unequivocal answer seems difficult to offer without endangering the complexities of the intertextual process. Arguably, intertextuality has a disruptive impact on mimetic procedures. Apart from indicating its postmodern affinities, this is also a pointer to the fact that 'we may have found a different... means to discuss perennial matters of allusion, reference, parody, and imitation' (O'Donnell xiii).

One possible way of looking at the issue is that intertextuality, rather than dispense with imitation, shifts the focus of imitation from the world to the word, simultaneously engendering a strain of self-consciousness in the process. Like Plato in the *Republic*, it addresses the problem of originality in literature, but it does this by deliberately resorting to previous texts in order to produce new ones, which is a peculiarly postmodern (because subversive) gesture.

A digression becomes necessary at this juncture: here and elsewhere in this study, the use of the term 'postmodern', particularly as an adjective to categorise the Victorianist novels, requires to be expounded in some detail. The overlap in technique between modernism and postmodernism also necessitates this, in order that the essential differences between the two be recognised. For one, modernism is elitist and exclusive in its approach, whereas postmodernism is popular and participatory.

Brian McHale in *Postmodernist Fiction* identifies a more fundamental distinction between the two. According to him, the modernist dominant is 'epistemological', while the postmodernist is 'ontological' (McHale 9 10). Modernist fiction is concerned with questions such as 'What is there to be known; Who knows it?; How do they know it, and with what degree of certainty?; How is knowledge transmitted from one knower to another, and with what degree of reliability?... What are the limits of the knowable? And so on' (McHale 9). Postmodernist questions on the other hand bear on the ontology of the literary text and the world it projects:

> What is a world?; What kinds of world are there, how are they constituted, and how do they differ? What happens when different kinds of world are placed in confrontation, or when boundaries between worlds are violated?; What is the mode of existence of a text, and what is the mode of existence of the world (or worlds) it projects?; How is a projected world structured? And so on. (McHale 10)

These typically postmodern concerns make themselves felt insistently and explicitly in *FLW* and *Heathcliff*, and implicitly in *Possession*, *Angels and Insects*, *Tess*, and *WSS*. In the analysis of individual novels, some of the features they exhibit may appear to be modernist. Yet, we shall retain the descriptive epithet 'postmodern' rather than 'modern' because, Victorianist novels are situated closer to the postmodernist than to the modernist paradigm. Postmodernism resists the drive towards closure, and it is out of such a resistance that the Victorianist novels are born. In other words, the Victorianist novels owe their existence to the refusal to accept the plots or characters or issues of their Victorian predecessor-texts as settled or closed.

Why the Victorians?

This research into Victorianist novels is motivated by the need to consider the following questions:

a) Why approach the Victorians intertextually?
b) Why the Victorians? What makes the Victorian period interesting?

One possible answer to question a) is that intertextuality is the most appropriate literary mode in the postmodern repertoire of trying to understand the past. Such is the present clime of theoretical sophistication, that a naïve continuation or re-statement of the past is impossible. Many postmodern tactics such as self-reflexive allusions, centering the margins, challenging the illusion of coherence, the fragmentation of vision and form, are used with great aplomb in Victorianist novels. *FLW* is a classic example of metafiction; *Possession* is almost entirely a dialogue between various genre-defined texts; while *WSS*, despite being restricted by its allegiance to a single text, is anything but a straightforward, linear sequel.

Thus for instance, were we to take a look at Jean Rhys's novel, it becomes clear at the outset that *Jane Eyre* is only a pre-text (and arguably a pretext) for Rhys to advance her thesis. The relationship that the new novel has to the old is one of re-working rather than re-affirming.

Although it technically predates the postmodern movement, *WSS* is deconstructive in spirit, and takes the Victorian text apart rather than preserving it. Its approach to its *ur*-text is by way of rebuke. One way in which *WSS* does this is to turn the myth of the intrusive 'other woman' inside out. It shows how *Jane Eyre*, ironically enough, casts the legitimate wife into the role of the Other Woman, because she is a Creole, and bestows legitimacy on the governess Jane, who is acceptable (to Victorian readers) because she is white *and* British. Jean Rhys revises Bertha's role and establishes her need for sympathy, not condemnation or imprisonment in the top storey of Rochester's mansion. *WSS* takes upon itself an almost moral responsibility for 'righting' a lopsided view. Its preoccupation with margins and boundaries is seen in the spotlight it throws on the outsider, and gives her a voice: she being trebly dispossessed as a woman, a non-Briton and mentally deranged.

Stephen Greenblatt suggests an entry into the Victorian question by declaring that 'in fact continual refashioning is at the center of the profession of literary study: it is both a characteristic of the texts we study and a crucial means to keep those texts and our own critical practices from exhaustion and sterility' (Greenblatt 5). A specific pointer towards intertextuality and its pivotal role in refashioning activities is made a little later, when he says, 'the goal in literary studies is not to seal off the frontier completely but to keep it conceptually alive: what is sought are not closed boundaries but regulated thresholds, controlled passageways' (Greenblatt 8). An interesting coincidence lies in the incarnation that this metaphor achieves in a fairy tale of that title in *Possession*.

The Victorians have effortlessly ensconced themselves into the postmodern milieu which, surprisingly enough, has turned out to be favourable to them. At least two major postmodern theoretical schools of the twentieth century, feminism and deconstruction, have depended extensively on Victorian texts to define themselves. Notions such as textual instability and deferral, peculiar to the postmodernists, have found admirable illustrations within Victorian texts, and 'the very literature that postmodernism first defined itself *against* turns out on such readings to be either proto-postmodernist or the authentic thing' (Levine 142, emphasis mine). Victorian literature has been revealed as not 'dated' by any means; that the Victorian text-corpus yields meanings appropriate to theoretical climes a century ahead, is a sign of its positive 'belatedness'.

Does this imply that the Victorians were actually postmodernists, and if so, does this dissolve their individuality? This question may be answered by suggesting that Victorian novels contain the potential to be analysed from a postmodern perspective. Victorianist novels like *Tess* and *WSS* depend on the Victorian identity of their parent texts, against which they define their own; their identity is contingent upon the independent and different existence of their progenitor-texts. In the final analysis, Victorianist intertextuality is an illustration of the postmodern tendency to construct 'fictional pieces around theoretical problems and issues' (Rowe 187).

On question b), 'Why the Victorians', it seems logical that the questions of the twentieth century be addressed to the nineteenth, with which it is historically contiguous. The Victorian spirit is essentially one of restless, if also reluctant interrogation. Much as they craved the reassurance of social and religious security, the Victorians could not find a conventional way out of the doubts and threats posed by Darwin's theory of natural selection. Doubts such as, whether the Bible was the Word of God, or only the record of man, troubled and teased them. Related anxieties such as the existence of a God at all have been inherited by the twentieth century.

Indeed the unsettling nature of questions which have no answers, which the Victorians were compelled to face, has become a natural property of the twentieth century. Due to shared Victorian and modern preoccupations, the 'Victorian past' gains precedence over others, and one may even see the two centuries as one continuum. Centuries, after all, are but convenient historical constructions.

Another likely answer to b) is that the novel is not only the characteristic Victorian genre, but the pre-eminent twentieth-century literary mode as well (Kundera 13). John Barth indicates this in 'The Literature of Replenishment' in *The Friday Book* (193–206). Victorianist novels become doubly interesting since they use the novel form to understand and re-assess the major literary vehicle of Victorian expression. Hidden issues like whether the novel has changed since then are for the reader to ponder over.

There has been an 'extraordinary increase in interest in things Victorian within the academy during the last twenty-five years', claims George Levine (130). The case for Victorianism is argued further by Bakhtin's choice of a classic Victorian novel, *Little Dorrit*, to elaborate his dialogic theory, which is a cornerstone of intertextuality.

The Victorian period has a beginning and an ending that is inextricably associated with its name – the ascension of Queen Victoria to the monarchy in 1837 and her death in 1901. This classification must necessarily be elastic, since Carlyle's *Sartor Resartus*, a classic Victorian text, was published in 1833. Yet, within this reductionist framework of dates, there lies a whole network of happenings which have been codified by common consent as 'Victorian': the Industrial Revolution, the Utilitarian movement, Darwinian revelations and the resultant loss of faith (Levine 133).

In choosing the Victorian text corpus for their inspiration and theme, authors of Victorianist novels circumvent the hurdle of subject matter. John Barth's essay, 'The Literature of Exhaustion' in *The Friday Book*, suggests this by citing re-play or re-readability as a literary touchstone. Victorianist novels stretch this idea further: if literary classics are universal in their appeal and lasting in their readability-value, then would these qualities empower them to be re-used as well as re-read? The Victorianist novels seem to affirm this possibility.

This possibility appears to be realised by the fact that the Victorian literary texts, which are chosen as resources, are classics, like *Tess of the d'Urbervilles*, *Jane Eyre*, 'Mr Sludge, "the Medium" ' or 'Goblin Market'. In some senses, then, the Victorianist novels preserve the traditional canon of literature, and perform a highly elitist act, laying claim simultaneously to the domains of creative and critical literature[13]. By acknowledging 'Victorianness' in Dickens or Browning and not, say, Philip James Bailey, Victorianist novelists group themselves with the intelligentsia. In fact a two-way process is at work here: by choosing from the canon, these intertextual novels gain access into 'high' literature, while in turn they confirm the 'classic' status of the Victorian texts by incorporating them in their own re-workings.

When, after having taken recourse to the canon, the Victorianist novels question some of the sacred foundations of the canon, such as Hardy's feminist leanings, they veer towards the postmodernist end, by opening vistas from perceived lacunae. From the fixture of pronouncements that Hardy and Brontë make, for instance, Tennant and Rhys create fissures that encourage a semantic flow in a reverse direction: from signified to signifier.

In the following chapters, we shall look into the construction of the intertextual identities of these Victorianist novels in some detail. We shall study the various ways in which genre confers intertextual identity on a novel. Beginning with the dramatic monologue, the most structured of the genres of this study, we shall work through the progressively less rigid ballad, the fairy-tale and the romance genres in this respect, culminating in the most accommodating of all genres, the novel. Intertextual potential grows with the growing elasticity of the concerned genre and so the novel would tend to come last in a study of intertextuality in different genres. Moreover, it is not possible to draw attention to the amazing embedding capacity of the novel without previously contrasting it with the genres that it embeds within itself.

This study will then take a look at the role of gender in creating intertextual identity, and also at minor textual devices. In the conclusion, we shall look at further possibilities in this area of study.

In the process certain concepts are likely to engage the attention of the reader periodically. These relate to boundaries and their transgression; to the way attitudinal changes create a new text out of an old one, and to the way in which intertextuality is historically deterministic. These factors pave the way for textual self-consciousness, which is integral to the success of intertextuality.

NOTES

1 Intertextuality is a notion 'according to which, in keeping with the Saussurean model of language, no text is intelligible except in its differential relations with other texts'. John Drakakis quoted in Clayton and Rothstein, eds. *Influence and Intertextuality in Literary History* (Wisconsin: University Press, 1991) 192.

2 '*ur*-text' is the German term for an original version of a text, usually applied to a version that is lost and has to be reconstructed. However, in this book 'ur' is used to indicate the parent text which is subjected to intertextual dialogue. Thus for example, Hardy's (final published version of) *Tess of the d'Urbervilles* is the *ur*-text for Tennant's *Tess*. Similarly the Victorian socio-literary-cultural fabric becomes Fowles's *ur*-text in *FLW*.

3 The term is used by Louise Yelin, 'Cultural Cartography', *Victorian Newsletter* (81 Spr 1992) 40. I am also indebted to Dr Ranjit Nair for suggesting this term to me.

4 Tennant in *Tess* and Swift in *Ever After* strengthen the textual code of Lyme Regis by weaving their Victorian narratives too around this place.

5 By juxtaposing different genres and creating a variety of textual patterns on the page, the text encourages a rupture or break in the reading process. This in turn helps to turn the reader away from the world of illusion portrayed in the text and reflect on the reading activity. The breaks create a digression within and therefore without the text.

6 Riffaterre's attempt to define the 'textual nature' of a work of art leads him to perceive the text as 'always one of a kind, unique'. *Text Production*, trans. Terese Lyons. (New York: Columbia University Press, 1983) 2.

7 The Greek word from which the term 'trope' originates means 'turn' or 'turning', and thus indicates a change of sense. A trope is any literary or rhetorical device which consists of the use of words in other then their literal sense. Similes and metaphors are good examples of tropes.

8 Deictic otherness: deictics/deictic elements are those features of language which locate utterances temporally (with words like 'now' or 'later') and spatially (with words like 'here' or 'there'), thereby playing a significant role in narrative. These words go a long way in creating a mental image for the reader. In intertextual proceedings, deixis becomes an important presence because of the inherent tendency of intertextual novels to 'point elsewhere', usually to the past. Tropes function as economical as well as subtle means of demonstrating intertextuality, since they 'stand in' for other texts.

9 I say 'counter-intuitive', because the common direction is from life to text. Life, or phenomenological reality, is usually the inspiration for a work of art.

10 'Pastiche' is a literary composition characterised by scraps, parts and motifs from different sources. It is essentially a medley.

11 The notion of the stereotype has been expounded at length in Rukmini Bhaya Nair's 'The Pedigree of the White Stallion: Postcoloniality and Literary History' in *The Uses of Literary History*, ed. Marshall Brown (Durham: Duke University Press, 1995).

12 'Mimesis' is the Greek word for imitation. It is understood largely in the context of Aristotle's *Poetics*, where Aristotle defines tragedy as an 'imitation of an action, not mere mimicry but the selection, arrangement, and presentation of acts that reveal the relation of art and life' (quoted in Harry Shaw, *A Dictionary of Literary Terms* 240).

13 An objection to 'postmodern' could be made here for instance, on the ground that the postmodernist mission to dislodge the canon is noticeably absent in these novels. It is true that *Tess* challenges the canonical Hardy and his feminist agenda, but since it begins by accepting Hardy's canonical status, which it then sets out to dismantle, its attack is less subtle and more direct than is the wont of postmodernism. Moreover, postmodernist techniques usually involve little more than a sense of play and a baring of the writing game. But the presence of stereotypes precludes this possibility in Victorianist fiction and negates Derridean absence, for in these novels the stereotypes function as counters that refuse to disintegrate. Indeed Victorianist fiction requires these counters against which it comes into existence. From a different point of view, it is equally possible to see the Victorian counters as the twentieth-century novel's way of re-leasing itself by resorting to a usable past.

1 The Dramatic Monologue

Genre and Intertextuality

The place of genre in endowing a text with intertextual status is arguably the foremost among literary devices. Genres are literary types classified on the bases of the conventions of representation with which they depict reality, or the phenomenological world.

The notion of inheritance and perhaps, also, indebtedness, allies genre-bound writing to intertextual writing. Both these aspects of representation contest the possibility of complete originality in a literary text. When Heather Dubrow observes of genre that 'our recognition of a genre encourages us to relate whatever the work at hand is evoking to the experience portrayed in other works we have read in the same genre' (Dubrow 34), she may well be saying the same of intertextuality.

Genre sets a given work of art within a certified category of literary class, and ensures an appropriate mode of reading the text. This allies it to intertextual operations, which exist on the criterion of learned responses and prior reactions to texts. Not only does genre too promote studied responses, it also aids the intertextual experience because 'generic signals often draw attention to the fact that what we are encountering is a fiction, rather than, say, an actual transcription of a funeral oration or a conversation between lovers' (Dubrow 34).

Although a text may incorporate generic conventions merely to subvert them, Victorianist novels like *Possession* and *Tess* are scrupulously loyal to the vision of the genres they adopt. *Possession* does not parody the dramatic monologue; neither does *Tess* mock the conventions of the ballad. Rather they enlist the co-operation of these genres both in becoming intertextual and in orienting the Victorian to Victorianist. For these novels, the act of choosing a well-established genre and perpetuating it is an acknowledgement of the past. Literary history encourages the equation of specific genres with specific historical periods (such as of drama with the Elizabethan period in England), a formula that Byatt capitalises upon in *Possession*. Her induction of the dramatic monologue goes a long way towards creating the Victorian ethos of

Possession. Indeed historical predestination of this kind cannot be overlooked in any intertextual application of genre.

Victorianist novels readily employ generic juxtaposition as a means of promoting intertextuality. The example that comes most readily to mind is Byatt's use of the dramatic monologue in *Possession*. 'Especially interesting are the habits of what might be termed host genres, those forms one of whose roles is to provide a hospitable environment for the other form or forms that are regularly incorporated within them' (Dubrow 116). In its Victorianist manifestations, the novel flaunts its felicity as an embedding genre, gracefully accommodating its 'guest' genres and displaying an extensive hospitality.

This and the next two chapters attempt to validate this statement by discussing the modes of generic behaviour that establish intertextuality in Victorianist narratives. Beginning with the most sharply defined of the genres under study, namely the dramatic monologue, this study proceeds to examine the ballad, the fairy tale, the romance, and finally the novel, along with their respective potential for Victorianist intertextuality.

The Dramatic Monologue

The Victorianist novel practises at least two methods of genre-based intertextuality. One is the incorporation of a few characteristic generic features, such as mystery, supernatural elements, and romance, to suggest a ballad. The second is the inclusion of a whole genre with its structure intact, which then marks a boundary between itself and the rest of the novel. It is the latter strategy that Byatt adopts in the case of the dramatic monologue.

In projecting a plethora of genres, *Possession* stands in danger of disintegrating into a mere, if clever, catalogue. What saves it is Byatt's use of a central intertext in the dramatic monologue, which exerts a centripetal force, holding the novel together. This genre is doubly advantaged since it is typical of the Victorian period as well as the twentieth century, and thereby helps Byatt to mark her novel as Victorian as well as Victorianist.

There are two dramatic monologues of importance in *Possession*: 'Mummy Possest' and 'Swammerdam'. Their capacity to suggest a particular literary-historical period comes from their generic identity. The dramatic monologue reached its zenith in the Victorian period and especially in the poetry of Robert Browning. Now the two monologues in *Possession* are not written by a 'real' poet, who actually lived in the Victorian period. Ash, their author, is a fictional character, closely modelled on Robert Browning. Yet the power of these monologues to convey the authentic Victorian ethos is no whit reduced. Their validity as Victorian signifiers is retained by virtue of the genre they belong to, that they are dramatic monologues.

The Dramatic Monologue in *Possession:* Role as Subtext

The status of the dramatic monologue in relation to *Possession* is that of subtext as it is defined by Riffaterre: 'a story or episode embedded in the text and mirroring the whole' (Riffaterre, 'On Narrative Subtexts: Proust's Magic Lantern' 450)[1]. Narrative subtexts are especially valuable in voluminous narratives like *Possession* which demand much mental gymnastics from the reader and a large space of his memory.

The subtext is a passage that is applied like a refrain, and reclaimed at significant strategic junctures as an aid to memory. As defined by Riffaterre, the subtext belongs to the world of the narrative, and is not detached from the illusionary web of the story. The dramatic monologue, however, functions like a subtext *outside* the story of *Possession*, concentrating instead on drawing the reader away from the charms of the story to show that all texts are but constructs. It does this by locating the argument about art in 'Mummy Possest', and making this dramatic monologue a brilliantly executed exercise in self-reflexivity.

We have noted earlier that the dramatic monologue is a genre that suggests both the Victorian as well as Victorianist *zeitgeist*. This makes the form invaluable for Victorianist intertextuality. Robert Langbaum may well be speaking for Byatt when he declares, 'In an age where there is no valid moral principle for connecting the events, the literature that takes the modern situation into account must approximate the dramatic monologue' (Langbaum 226)[2]. 'Mummy Possest' is thus richly intertextual, by straddling two centuries as well as being self-reflexive. Its title comes from John Donne's 'Love's Alchymie': 'Hope not for minde in women; at their best/Sweetnesse and wit, they're but *Mummy*, Possest'. (*Possession* 299, Donne 86–87). As subtext, the dramatic monologue does not mirror the narrative of *Possession* so much as the form of *Possession,* which examines the status of art in the light of its many textual manifestations.

Definitions of the Dramatic Monologue

While literary historians unstintingly grant the pride of place to the dramatic monologue in Victorian literature, its semantic and connotative potential has not been adequately explored, owing to its codification in terms of purely technical features (Armstrong 13). To define the dramatic monologue as a poem, whose particular context is defined by a speaker, his intention, a silent listener, and an occasion, is to be guilty of reductionism. Armstrong's comprehensive definition of the dramatic monologue redresses this lack by actually perceiving it as a twentieth-century text in the values it enshrines.

> The extreme textual sophistication of the monologue or the dramatic lyric, a poem proposing itself as the immediacy of a speaking voice in dialogue with a silent listener, but which is in reality a text, a written artefact, raises immediately the problem of its own and the reader's status by confusing speaking, which assumes a listener's presence, with writing, which assumes an addressee's absence. (Armstrong 288)

Already, therefore, the dramatic monologue possesses two traditions — the oral and the written, within itself. This statement tacitly indicates that self-consciousness is a latent presence in the dramatic monologue. The reader reads a text constructed out of a speaker interpreting himself to a listener interpreting him, but who is only to be inferred from the subject's speech. There is an infinite regress of possible interpretive instability as the reader's own reading process is implicated in hermeneutic difficulty (Armstrong 288).

This has major implications for the kind of reading that a dramatic monologue demands: a reading between the lines. Although it is in the speaker that the monologue finds literal and metaphoric utterance, the listener is equally important in the dimension he provides to the dramatic monologue. Silence, which is the listener's medium, is as potent as language. Unlike the relatively impotent *reader*, the text-internal listener conditions the speaker's utterance more actively from within the form itself, than the reader, who is outside the artifice and entrenched in reality, can ever succeed in doing. This is because the reader is confronted with the text after it is a complete(d) entity, whereas the internal listener of the monologue participates in giving birth to the text.

The context thus participates in giving rise to metafiction, which is reinforced in the following way: the writer has to communicate a fictitious audience to his real one without allowing the former the liberty of utterance. The silent listener is represented at one remove through the speaker, but since the latter is not guileless, the validity of the listener's representation by the speaker is questionable. It rests on the poet to ensure that the speaker's voice does not assume a totalitarian authority. With so many points of view all claiming for expression, it is difficult for the reader not to move away from the content of the poem to its highly crafted structure, which is the first step towards self-reflexivity.

Like form, language too assumes complexity in the dramatic monologue because the speaker is usually trying to extricate himself from an embarrassing situation or justify his stance. The speaker in 'Mummy Possest' is an ideal example: her spuriousness is a legacy of the inherited tradition of the dramatic monologue. It is in the speaker's interest to convince his listener(s), both internal and external, of the validity of his position, and persuasive language is his only means of vindicating himself. Since his aim is to win his listeners over, an undercurrent of tension exists in the dramatic monologue. Robert Langbaum describes this inherent conflict as a struggle between 'sympathy' and 'judgement' (75), and suggests the way out of the two extremes by recommending a 'willing suspension of judgement' to understand the speaking character from his biased viewpoint.

The dramatic monologue compels a suspension of moral judgement because it inclines, particularly in Browning's versions of it, to present such unusual speakers as Porphyria's mad lover-murderer and the unscrupulous Duke of Ferrara in 'Porphyria's Lover' and 'My Last Duchess' respectively. Characters like these tend to intensify the tension between sympathy and evaluation on the reader's part. By creating what Langbaum calls impossible cases (Langbaum 86), whom the reader must accept, the dramatic monologue carves a difficult space for itself in the canon. This inherent tension in the dramatic monologue, along with its tendency to problematise truth, makes it an excellent vehicle to bridge the Victorian–Victorianist breach. Its refusal to spell either character or theme in black and white is a very postmodern attitude, where there is no truth, only truths.

Why the Dramatic Monologue?

In *Possession* nineteenth-century verse is duplicated with amazing authenticity primarily through the dramatic monologue; but Byatt must also show that the informing intelligence is twentieth-century and postmodernist. There being no dispute about the dramatic monologue being prototypically Victorian, the question that needs to be asked is, how is the dramatic monologue suitable for representing the twentieth century?

The layered structure of this genre enables it to be self-reflexive in a way that few other genres (except perhaps the novel) are, and also enables it to present points of view rather than truth. To recapitulate, then, both self-consciousness and the predominance of points of view over an absolute conclusion are typically postmodern, and characteristic of the twentieth-century mode of apprehending reality. Browning's favourite poetic form is thus naturally gifted with a capacity for self-examination; its preoccupation with language and artistic creativity is foregrounded also through a debate on art in 'Mr Sludge, "the Medium" ' from *Dramatis Personae* as well as 'Mummy Possest'.

The epigraph in *Possession* selects precisely those self-reflexive observations from 'Mr Sludge, "the Medium" ' that endow it with a postmodern sensibility:

> How build such solid fabric out of air?
> How on so slight foundation found this tale,
> Biography, narrative? or, in other words,
> 'How many lies did it require to make
> The portly truth you here present us with?'
>
> ('Mr Sludge "The Medium" ', quoted in *Possession* as epigraph, 157–58, ll 1458–62)

The second postmodern feature of the dramatic monologue, the struggle between two or more voices, may be illustrated from 'Mummy Possest', which has at least two instances of the text escaping the power of the speaker in order to work against her. The first act of textual insubordination occurs when she unwittingly blurts out that her mediumistic practice is lucrative, and then tries in vain to modify the meaning: 'Most *promising* – that is, in spiritual terms –' (*Possession* 407, emphasis mine).

In the second case, the speaker ultimately brings herself to give professional secrets away to Geraldine. At this juncture, her confidence is eroded to the extent of letting the text reveal her discomfiture in confessing to fraudulent practices. She wants to claim that if they improvise they do so in the interests of truth. But she falters thrice before asserting this lie, and repeats the phrase, 'I tell you this' three times ('I tell you this because – I tell you this – / In fine, I tell you this'), before she can gain sufficient command over the text to impose her version on it (*Possession* 407). This repetition signals her loss of control over the text for a brief while, and the pauses show her lack of confidence in what she is about to state. As a mode of articulating doubt, the dramatic monologue becomes a fitting cultural reflection not only of Victorian times, but also of the postmodern clime.

Concerns of the Dramatic Monologue: Truth, Falsehood, Imagination, and Representation

The dramatic monologue's understanding of the problematic of apprehending truth is demonstrated even in a Victorian (as opposed to Victorianist) text such as Robert Browning's *The Ring and the Book* (1868–69). In itself an intertextual work, this collection of dramatic monologues provides varying descriptions of the truth in reproducing the account of a Renaissance Italian murder. Browning's *ur*-text is 'The Yellow Book' which draws a clear distinction between the good (innocent) and the bad (guilty) persons involved in the crime. Browning however confuses the black-and-white report of 'The Yellow Book' by having a) different persons see different 'truths' of the matter and b) the same person (Guido Franceschini) tell a different truth at two different points in time. In this intent he is admirably aided by the dramatic monologue.

In the leeway it offers for an academic exercise in the representation of truth, the dramatic monologue enables both writer and reader 'to participate in a position to see what it feels like to believe that way, without having finally to agree' (Langbaum 105)[3]. It thus engages with the problem of a) a multiplicity of meanings b) struggling to express themselves through c) a voice struggling (in the opposite direction) to keep (the illusion of) unity. This layered structure causes the dramatic monologue to be heavily ironic. Sperber and Wilson's definition suggests how irony can be operative in the dramatic monologue: 'Irony plays on the relationship between the speaker's thought and a thought of someone other than the speaker' (Sperber and Wilson 243). Also, 'Genuine irony is echoic' (Sperber and Wilson 241), and embedded in an ironic statement is an attitude referring to a previous utterance. There is an apt illustration from 'Mummy Possest', where the speaker quite obviously echoes Geraldine's hesitation sarcastically: 'What's that you say? You do not like to lie?' (*Possession* 408). Here the speaker, through mere repetition, ridicules Geraldine's moral scruples. As the poem progresses, the speaker gradually asserts her power over Geraldine and makes it impossible for the latter to speak further on the subject.

In a dramatic monologue irony proves to be of value because the listener's response has necessarily to be conveyed by the speaker. In conveying this, the speaker inevitably colours it with his attitude, be it disapproval or mockery. Since struggle is the textual pattern of a dramatic monologue, the speaker and the listener rarely offer mutual approbation. As a metalinguistic trope that can generate several interpretations from one utterance, irony is a natural feature of the dramatic monologue. Its dependence on echoing allies it to intertextual procedures, which also involve a repetition qualified by an attitude.

At this stage, a closer look is warranted at the individual monologues whose voices shape the intertextual design of *Possession*. These include real and counterfeit ones, and both Victorian as well as Victorianist poems. The first in chronological survey is *Tennyson's Maud: A Monodrama* (1855). Maud Bailey is the name of a twentieth-century university lecturer in Byatt's novel. The course of the plot reveals the Victorian poet Ash to be her ancestor, but her literary kinship is with Tennyson, as affirmed in the words used to describe her. Her personality, in Tennyson's words, is 'icily regular, splendidly null' (*Possession* 316,

506). This kind of description is characterised by an inversion of the norm; here the 'real' world within *Possession* derives its semantic significance from literature instead of the more common reverse operation. Life does not enrich text so much as text enriches life. This notion will be elaborated on in the chapter, 'The Novel'.

A dramatic monologue of secondary importance to 'Mummy Possest' in *Possession* is 'Swammerdam' (*Possession* 202–9). Though in Ash's literary mythology, Swammerdam is the discoverer of the microscope, Swammerdam was actually a seventeenth-century biologist who was 'possessed' with an insatiable curiosity to collect, dissect and find order through microscopic organisms. His classifications and catalogues eventually lead him to the realisation that the source of all life, whether of a man or of an insect, is one. 'The more the Many were revealed to me,/The more I pressed my hunt to find the One', says Swammerdam, and like Darwin, 'sought to know the origins of life' (*Possession* 206).

Besides complicating the dividing lines between illusion and reality (a popular device for promoting self-reflexivity) by having a fictitious poet (Ash) write about a 'real' historical character (Swammerdam), Byatt thematically invests 'Swammerdam' with the pursuit of truth. Swammerdam's quest for the truth leads to the realisation that truth eludes man's finitude. In the final analysis, truth can only be suggested through paradoxes which defeat logic, and can be apprehended only in terms of perspective: 'The optic lens is a slicing sword./It multiplies the world, or it divides' (*Possession* 207). The optic lens is a fortuitous metaphor to use, since this refers not only to the microscope that Swammerdam uses for his work, but also to the kind of perspective-glass that the dramatic monologue requires its reader to wear. This metaphor becomes a paradigm for the structure of the dramatic monologue itself, as it describes its operations: 'We see the many in the one, as here,/We see the segments of what once seemed smooth' (*Possession* 207).

The Real and the Counterfeit: 'Mr Sludge, "The Medium"' and 'Mummy Possest'

The relationship between the monologues of Browning and Ash warrant close scrutiny. The similarities between 'Mr Sludge, "The Medium"' and 'Mummy Possest', being comparatively fewer than the differences, let us begin with them first:

a) Both end on a note of deceit, which remains the final and lasting impression of the monologue.
b) Both define their positions against their respective authors' personal prejudices, for both Browning and Ash mistrusted séances.

c) Both are written in the iambic pentameter; this stylistic identity reinforces their thematic similarity.

The differences between them are rather pronounced:

a) In 'Mummy Possest' the speaker is a female. Despite resorting to deception she speaks with the confidence and authority of someone in power. She is therefore able to present her 'vocation' in a flattering light. Her confidence derives from the relative powerlessness of her listener, Geraldine.

   The speaker in 'Mr Sludge', on the other hand, is male. His position is threatened, and his voice is therefore pleading, grovelling, cajoling, wheedling, and occasionally defiant. Since Sludge has to justify his cheating despite his powerless position, he cannot present a heroic picture of himself: 'Tread on a worm, it turns, sir!' ('Mr Sludge "the Medium"' *Dramatis Personae* 115)

b) The speaker in Ash's monologue equivocates about fraud when she does not repudiate it totally. Sludge is forced to admit that he has been cheating since he is caught in the act.

c) Probably due to the equations of power between the speakers and their silent listeners within the two poems, 'Mummy Possest' is less dialogic in spirit than 'Mr Sludge', because the speaker's authority is greater here. 'Mr Sludge' emerges as a more dynamic poem because of the almost palpable tussle of emotions in Sludge, as well as the delicate balance of his 'dealings' with Horsefall who has exposed him.

d) The images in 'Mummy Possest' tend to describe the practice of literature as well as spiritualism in congratulatory terms: 'Now see/The shifting *lights* move on the stones' and 'A spider-web of *light*'. (*Possession* 405, emphasis mine). On the other hand, 'Mr Sludge' has unsavoury and unattractive images such as the medium's reference to himself as a worm.

e) 'Mummy Possest' is intertextual with i) Browning's 'Mr Sludge, "the Medium" '; and ii) Donne's 'Loves Alchymie'[4]; whereas 'Mr Sludge' is a self-contained text.

f) There are also stylistic differences. Unlike 'Mr Sludge, "the Medium" ', which employs inverted commas to represent the responses of the silent listener, 'Mummy Possest' does not highlight the listener's reactions. Also it has no 'asides'; 'Mr Sludge' has many.

g) Finally, 'Mummy Possest' is a short(er) poem (than 'Mr Sludge, "the Medium" ', which is 1,525 lines long). The latter ends, unlike 'Mummy Possest', with a soliloquy. This can incidentally promote a reading of 'Mr Sludge' as an inter-generic text.

The following textual excerpts show the crucial point of meeting between the two poems.

> . . . so Sludge lies!
> Why, he's at worst your poet who sings how Greeks
> That never were, in Troy which never was,
> Did this or the other impossible great thing
>
> ('Mr Sludge, "The Medium" ' 157,
> ll 1435–38, quoted in *Possession*)

and

> Art tells a truth, sweet girl, though all her tales
> Are lies i' the law-court, or the chemist's phial-
>
> 'Mummy Possest' (*Possession* 409)

The séance-medium is analogous to the poet since the medium gives voice to spirits that exist beyond the human world. The notion of an inspired medium intertextually recalls Sidney's divine *Vates* ('An Apology for Poetry' 6) and before him, Plato's frenzied poet, whose utterances were basically epiphanic and born out of inspired moments. This reading is supported in the novel by its title, 'Possession'. The concept of a medium is interesting to study, particularly in the fact that it is not so important in itself as in its role of a conduit. What it conveys is of greater significance than itself. Ideally, the medium aspires to a state of transparency in order to deflect attention away from itself. This process is observed in the medium of the séance as well as the medium of writing, which is language. The pun on the word 'medium' is significant in understanding the impact of Byatt's argument.

When Browning and Ash foreground the medium, they centre attention on textuality and language by relying on the pun inherent in the word 'medium', as well as by the debate on art which both poems foster. The reader's attention is drawn through the human medium conducting the séance to the language-medium, which is supposedly used by poets as a means of perpetrating falsehood. Reflexivity (rather than reflection or imitation) becomes an issue in both monologues, and the problem of defining artistic creativity thus leads to a discussion of what textuality entails.

Metafictional discussions on the nature of art in both monologues are contextualised in the séance. The strictures on art are delivered by the medium in both cases, but the integrity of these mediums is more or less eroded by the revelation that they are spurious. Meanwhile, there is also a biographical angle that needs to be reckoned with, that Browning as well as Ash mistrusted mediums. These angles contribute to the layered structure and struggle of both the monologues. The most obvious statement appears to be, if poets are like mediums and if mediums are liars, the poet's world too is false and ridden with lies. However, the postmodern temper of *Possession* cautions against the formulation of a simplistic statement such as this. With various qualifications in mind the reader has to arrive at a definition of art in both poems. The crux of the issue is that Browning and Ash disliked mediums, yet they chose to present a vindication of the poet's art through them. The implications of this may be one or more of the following:

a) That Browning and Ash think meanly of poetry; which, however, is a self-defeating conclusion to arrive at. This is the most unlikely possibility, and the very naivete of its assumption is an insult to the intricately crafted structure of the dramatic monologue.
b) That they are highlighting the problematic of establishing literary and artistic value by ruing that such a noble vocation as art is forced to rely on intrinsically dishonest voices.
c) Conversely, that this lofty calling can establish its value despite insincere votaries for it. Artistic value remains unsullied by the unflattering comparisons it is subjected to. This interpretation makes a high claim for the invulnerability of artistic worth.
d) That they demonstrate how language, which is (also) a medium (of expression), is inadequate to describe truth. The statement that art has to contend with frauds like Sludge who audaciously depict their cheating practices in terms of artistic creativity, is an observation that is wholly deconstructive in spirit and made structurally effective through the dramatic monologue.

The second hypothesis is self-evident, therefore it is necessary to move further on and examine (c) and (d) in some detail. Are Browning and Ash trying to establish the intrinsic greatness of literature by playing the devil's advocate? An affirmative answer to this question is undermined by the temper of postmodernism, which does not subscribe to idealistic views of art. The process of encountering and perceiving instability as inevitable has grown and intensified in the postmodern clime, where values such as artistic 'greatness' are not readily accepted.

The last possibility is the most powerful implication, and it also enlarges the scope of the dramatic monologue from Victorian to Victorianist. The monologues of Browning and Ash depend on their formal structure to disavow judgement(s) on artistic value, and refuse to evoke ethics as a criterion. They indicate that only statements about the nature of art are possible, and this is indeed a teleological conclusion of literary history. Byatt's deployment of the ventriloquism metaphor elsewhere in *Possession* reinforces the idea that the reader has to consider a myriad voices without ever reaching the one absolutely truthful voice that he can count upon. The fact that each of the voices in the text gives way before the next, like a kaleidoscope displaying different designs from different angles, ensures that there is no single, fundamental text in the dramatic monologue. Each voice is precariously poised on the boundary of the next. While this could testify to the protean nature and unreliability of all art, it could equally support an interpretation of art as uniquely multi-dimensional.

The voices in 'Mr Sludge, "the Medium" ' and 'Mummy Possest' act like Derrida's signifiers, deferring endlessly without arriving; one is qualified by another and then by a third. Complexity is intensified since at least two of the voices are silent: those of the poet and the fictitious listener. The monologues belie their name by being extremely polyphonic and permitting, like the novel, plural perspectives. Although Isobel Armstrong suggests that this results in a democratisation of the genre (Armstrong 143), it in fact results in a power-play within the logistics of the text, lending weight to her prior definition of a text as 'struggle' (Armstrong 10).

Let us look at some of the possible permutations. A passive listener like Geraldine (and unlike Horsefall) who succumbs to the perspective of the speaker will be gradually silenced even as the speaker's voice gains in strength. Moreover, the listener can be represented only through the speaker, whose motives are selfish. The speaker has the opportunity to misrepresent his listener's stance, and an unscrupulous protagonist like Ash's female medium can be trusted to take unfair advantage of the situation. If, in addition, the poet's voice is in disharmony with the speaker's as in 'Mr Sludge, "the Medium" ' and 'Mummy Possest', the reader is left holding a seethingly active text whose field is constantly shifting.

The wrestling between viewpoints is not resolved by Byatt, whose chief concern is to problematise it in Browning's as well as her Ash's text. The entire issue revolves around the role of imagination, which forms a threshold from the realm of truth to that of lies. Products of the imagination, such as literature, appear to be synonymous with falsehood.

And lying itself undergoes a promotion in the hierarchy of ethics as Sludge and Ash's speaker condone falsehood on the dubious ground that things are made better, sorrows more bearable by lying. The question remains, whether the poetic imagination takes one to a plane of higher truth or to one of falsehood, when it abjures a fidelity to facts. There is no final answer to the riddle except, perhaps, acquiescence in Sludge's defence that as a medium he commits fraud for the sake of his listeners, who prefer comfortable lies to hard truth. By implying complicity, the onus of the blame is transferred to the reader.

NOTES

1 'The subtext is born fully armed like Minerva from Jupiter's forehead. . . Even though an embedding necessarily appears in compressed form because, despite being a unit of significance, it must remain subordinate to the sequence of which it is a component, the embedded complex must contain fragments of the larger wholes that would be its components if that complex were allowed full development': Michael Riffaterre, 'On Narrative Subtexts: Proust's Magic Lantern' *Style* (22, 3, 1988) 454.

2 This disclosure prompts Isobel Armstrong to designate Browning as a Derridean before his time in *Victorian Poetry* (London: Routledge, 1993) 295.

3 This raises a fresh problem: if truth varies for different people, what credentials does art hold in order to report (a) truth? The argument about art, truth and artistic truth goes back in time to Plato, for whom art was synonymous with falsehood (354). Browning further complicates the issue by choosing such a form as the dramatic monologue to talk about truth. Moreover Sludge is a master of negotiatory tactics and so is the speaker in 'Mummy Possest'; both prevaricate on the nature of art and its relationship to truth. Elsewhere Browning himself raises the question in the guise of an impartial narrator, only to give an idealistic answer: 'Why take the artistic way to prove so much?/Because, it is the glory and good of Art, /That Art remains the one way possible/Of speaking truth, to mouths like mine at least' (*The Ring and the Book* 509, ll 837–40). This is a provocative claim, but in the Victorian milieu, where religious certainties had collapsed and a substitute was being desperately sought, Browning was indicating the same role for art that Arnold envisaged in 'The Study of Poetry'.

4 The reference is helpfully provided by James Blackadder, a character in *Possession* (London: Vintage, 1990) 299.

2 *The Ballad, the Fairy Tale and the Romance*

This chapter discusses three genres, two of which, the ballad and the romance, are independent in their own right. Yet they are grouped together here on the basis of certains hared characteristics. The fairy tale, which borrows many of the features of the romance, is included for the same reason in this discussion.

The Ballad

The intertextual function of the ballad is admirably illustrated in Emma Tennant's Victorianist narrative *Tess*, which reproduces the ballad in the garb of a novel. In adopting a pre-eminently recitative genre like the ballad, Tennant is also compelled to engage with the question of orality, which she responds to by collapsing the barriers between oral discourse, ballad, and feminism. The contextual field of *Tess* groups itself into two categories as the story unwinds. The first is that of the prose ballad, whose narrator manipulates the reader-listener into acknowledging the ballad-like qualities of Hardy's story. The second is feminism, which marks itself as a definitive twentieth-century critical school. It is the feminist voice that challenges Hardy's benevolent fatherhood in the creation of Tess, and accuses him of collusion in her tragic destiny. Equally it is the feminist voice that marks *Tess* as a Victorianist novel.

Tennant's inclusion of the politics of gender into her narrative deserves undivided and separate attention, which will be dealt with in the chapter, 'Gender and Intertextuality'. The focus here is on Tennant's use of genre in the re-presentation of *Tess of the d'Urbervilles*. She appropriately settles on the ballad as her chosen genre as it enables her to achieve two goals simultaneously. As a narrative form, it justifies the re-telling of Hardy's story, since ballads are characterised by repetition, and repetition of various sorts. The typical ballad carries a refrain that is echoed periodically through it; here we have one kind of repetition. This apart, ballads require repetition in order to survive, and be transmitted from generation to generation. At the same time, the ballad also effortlessly accommodates the feminist cause, since story-telling, as Tennant establishes, is an inherently female activity.

As Liza-Lu, one of the characters poetically describes, 'Like the tapestries, embroideries and patchworks which carried the message of our anonymous love or suffering, the oral tradition of telling stories was our great, unsigned charter' (Tennant 48). The term 'charter' conveys a sense of ownership and authority, while the similes could not be more appropriate, belonging as they do to the discourse of textile, suggesting texture as well as textuality. In keeping with Liza-Lu's observation, Tennant traces the source of Hardy's stories to those that he heard his mother tell. His favourite theme of unhappy and unrequited love is patently ballad-like, and belongs to the repertoire of the oral narrative tradition. Although technically the ballad-singer may be male, like Hardy himself, the spirit and legacy of this genre are feminine. This point is emphasised in the narrative structure of *Tess,* which is in the form of a ballad sung by a grandmother to a baby girl.

Tennant's introduction of the features of the ballad-form in *Tess* shows dexterity and creative adventure. Unlike Byatt who clearly maintains the structural differences between the novel and the dramatic monologue in *Possession*, and lets an intertextual dialogue ensue between them, Tennant blurs the formal difference between the novel and the ballad. She does this by calling her novel 'a ballad' throughout the text, instead of, say, incorporating a ballad within the framework of her novel, which is Byatt's way of achieving intertextuality. In fact Tennant's technique is similar to Byatt's approach to the romance, which is the subtitle she gives *Possession*. Such an assimilation of a new genre within the novel results in a blurring of rigid generic demarcations, and even if the new genre is not completely interchangeable with the novel, the lines become difficult to draw. The conventions of the ballad used by Tennant help the reader to view the novel as a transparent genre behind which lies the essentially balladic *Tess*.

Features of the Ballad in *Tess*

'The ballad poet drew his materials from community life, from local and national history, from legend and folklore. His tales are usually of adventure, war, love, death and the supernatural' (Cuddon 72).

The most striking ballad-feature in *Tess* relates to theme. It contains four of the five features listed by Cuddon. Tragedy is natural to the ballad, and the tragic nature of the Tess story is confirmed by both versions, the Victorian version provided by Hardy as well as the Victorianist provided by Tennant. Secondly, a single narrative thread and speedy progression of events which characterise ballads, are to be found in *Tess*. Both these generic features preclude an in-depth treatment of character in the ballad, and appropriately enough, personae in *Tess* are presented in a few bold strokes and summarily dispensed with. Here the intertextual status of the novel helps Tennant admirably. The names ('Tess', 'Alec', 'Liza-Lu') alone are sufficient to indicate character because they have Victorian counterparts. Thirdly, ballads are commonly grouped into Primary or Folk Ballads, and Secondary or Literary Ballads. *Tess* equivocates by belonging to both categories. The 'story' of Tess is as old as the Celts; yet it remained anonymous and marginal until its folk-identity had been transmuted into a literary one by Hardy.

Apart from these basic features, the ballad identity of *Tess* is reaffirmed in the formal categories that Tennant adopts. The most striking of these is an oral and immediate transmission, represented through the mode of a direct address. Tennant simulates this by using the second person pronoun, 'you'. This unusual stylistic device goes a long way towards grounding *Tess* in the oral tradition. The entire novel is presumed to be a song sung to baby Tess, right from: 'The minute I saw you I knew you belong to the first lot' (Tennant 3), to 'Two minutes more to tell you, Ella, and Baby Tess' (Tennant 209). The ballad is in fact intended to be sung rather than spoken; it is 'transmitted from *singer* to *singer* by word of mouth' (Cuddon 70, emphasis mine). Examples from *Tess* follow:

> "You've heard the ballad" (Tennant 185);
> "Or may be he's extra sensitive and he's heard the ballad of Tess that I *sung* to you when no one else is about," (Tennant 148, emphasis mine);
>
> ". . . made it official that the ballad of Tess should be *sung* through the female of the species –" (Tennant 173, emphasis mine);
>
> "And I'll *sing* out the rest of the ballad to you"
> (Tennant 201, emphasis mine)

and

> 'Do some women, by entering a compact with the writer of the old ballad – the *song* of betrayal after love, of revenge and murder and death – carry the *song* to the next generation by accident almost,. . . ."
> (Tennant 206, emphases mine)

In Hardy's novel Tess Durbeyfield recalls the ballad her mother used to sing, of the mystic robe 'That never would become that wife/ That had once done amiss' (*Tess of the d'Urbervilles* 203).

It has previously been observed that the refrain is a major distinguishing feature of the ballad. 'A phrase, line or lines repeated at intervals during a poem and especially at the end of a stanza. . . . Very often it is an exact repetition. Sometimes it serves to work out an 'argument' in a poem, in which case it will undergo slight modifications. . .' says Cuddon of the refrain (559). At least half-a-dozen examples of the refrain can be furnished from *Tess*:

> "The chain of passion, betrayal and revenge goes on" (Tennant 25)

> ". . . and the old ballad, sung since the ending of that natural way - the ballad of love, seduction, betrayal. . . and, just sometimes, revenge-" (Tennant 34)

> ". . . he sees, under the quiet, peace and domesticity which is the smiling face of England, its recurring theme of cruelty, murder, reprisal and revenge" (Tennant 58)

> "The cycle of love, betrayal and revenge has been caught again, and will be set down for posterity by Thomas Hardy, progenitor and lover of Tess" (Tennant 121)

> "Then Tess, any Tess, can come after he has gone – to act out the story of love, revenge, betrayal and death". (Tennant 157)

Tess of the d'Urbervilles and *Tess* both authenticate the refrain, but *Tess* does this in a more self-conscious manner. Alongside, the reader is also made aware of another factor in these refrains – what one may term the feminine factor. The most common issue in ballads is sexuality. Male–female relations are the thematic centres of ballads, and Hardy's and Tennant's 'ballads' both confirm this pattern.

In the exercises described thus far, Tennant's exertions in drawing the ballad into her novel are ingenious but simple. Her real problem lies in the fact that the ballad is essentially a poetic form. There exists a metrical divide between prose and poetry, which cannot be closed by Tennant without doing considerable violence to received literary conventions. She partially overcomes this hurdle by allowing her definition of the ballad to merge with the most fundamental understanding of it as a narrative. By stressing such factors such as plot and theme, and incorporating stylistic devices such as the refrain, she succeeds in endowing a prose story with the identity of a ballad despite the anomaly of a metrical absence.

One of the distinguishing marks of the ballad is the ballad metre. This is traditionally 'a four-line stanza or quatrain containing alternating four-stress and three-stress lines. The rhyme scheme is usually *abcb*; sometimes *abab*' (Cuddon 73). Although this cannot feature in the novel *Tess,* a prose equivalent for it is discovered in the 'chapter'. Conventionally, each chapter marks the beginning of a new stage in the narrative after the previous section comes to an end. Tennant experiments by modelling her chapters on the ballad-stanza so that they are short and summary. Moreover, individual chapters have internal breaks, which enhance the impression of brevity.

A particularly noteworthy feature in *Tess* is Tennant's brilliant use of the enjambment, which is basically a poetic technique. This device entails the extension of one line without either a formal or a semantic interruption into the next line, the two lines being the last line of one stanza and the first line of the following stanza. In itself, the enjambment typifies the intertextual act of boundary-crossing in microcosmic proportions. The enjambment disrupts the traditional unity of a stanza by suggesting that one stanza has to reach out to another for both to be complete. There is an exchange, a negotiation if you will, between two conventionally self-contained units.

Keeping in mind that it is the chapter which officiates for the stanza in *Tess*, the employment of the enjambment here involves boundary-crossing on a large-scale dimension. Take for instance, page 9 of the novel:

> Where you are now, in the last season of the last year of the millennium—and where we were then, on that hot September day in 1954. And long before that and ever since, too,
>
> on
>
> # Chesil Bank[1]
>
> Chesil bank is one of the geological wonders of the world.

Here we have a sentence (instead of a line) running out from the end of a chapter into the beginning of the next.

Tennant's resourceful deployment of the present tense in her narrative, instead of the usual simple past, signposts the presence of the ballad in her story. Ballads usually convey an immediacy of effect in the impression they leave on their reader, which is one of breathless, racy happening. Even though the story may have happened long ago, its retelling is effected in such a manner as to make the story come alive for the duration of the narration. In *Tess*, the present tense helps Tennant to achieve a constant immediacy of effect. To take just one instance, Liza-Lu who recapitulates Tess's pregnancy and her unwed state, re-lives and reports the event as though it occurs right then, rather than being drawn from memory (Tennant 30).

An element of suspense survives[2] the intertextual borrowings of Tennant and imparts a sense of urgency to the story. The reader is informed at an early stage that a murder has been committed, and the body hidden away. Although no clue is provided about the identity of the murdered person, the reader is likely to surmise that the body is Alec's, deducing from Hardy. In Hardy's *Tess of the d'Urbervilles* the only murder that takes place is that of Alec, whom Tess kills. But Tennant breaks the narratorial allegiance to Hardy at this juncture in the plot by revealing, at the very end, Tess's father John Hewitt to be the murdered man. Here she actually depends upon the mystery in the earlier novel to lead the reader of her novel astray, till she springs her surprise on him.

Intertextuality implies a kind of predestination, since the forerunning novel has made many of the successor novel's choices in the spheres of plot, theme, characterisation and perhaps genre. Yet this does not close all doors for the later novel. Within this space there is still freedom to make further, if limited choices. For Tennant this task is not just challenging but also crucial, as becomes evident in her choice of John Hewitt as the murdered man. In Tennant's case, the reader may even assume the identity of the dead man to be of no consequence, since Tennant has made her feminist point without 'murdering' Alec. Whereas for Hardy, the justified murder of Alec was one of the high-points of his avowed feminism. But Tennant has her reasons for changing the identity of the murdered person: she shows that Tess's father, not lover, is the one who has sexually abused her. Furthermore, Hewitt is murdered not by Tess, but by her mother. This twist to the original plot of *Tess* (*Tess of the d'Urbervilles*) enables Tennant to accuse Hardy, who is Tess's literary 'father', as equally deserving of murder.

Finally, like the romance, the ballad requires an ambience all its own to make an impact on its reader–listener. The supernatural element is 'natural' to the world of the ballad. One locates this in *Tess of the d'Urbervilles*, in the story that Angel Clare tells Tess about the legend of the d'Urberville coach (210–11). He begins the tale but leaves it unfinished and much later, Alec d'Urberville completes it for her:

> this sound of a non-existent coach can only be heard by one of d'Urberville blood, and it is held to be of ill-omen to the one who hears it. It has to do with a murder, by one of the family, centuries ago. . . . One of the family is said to have abducted some beautiful woman, who tried to escape from the coach in which he was carrying her off, and in the struggle he killed her–or she killed him–I forget which. Such is one version of the tale. . . . (*Tess of the d'Urbervilles* 348)

This in itself constitutes an ideal story-line for a ballad. Tess has a vision of this coach and senses something uncanny about it. Despite seeing the carriage for the first time, she is nevertheless not able to rid herself of a disturbing conviction that she has seen it before, quite possibly in a dream (210).

Alec d'Urberville's reference to omens is a generic feature assimilated by Tennant. Omens, both good and ill, function as portents of the narrative course of the ballad. A cock that crows in the afternoon bodes ill. This becomes a significant omen in Hardy's as well as Tennant's texts. After their wedding Tess and Angel take their leave of Dairyman Crick and others on their way to Wellbridge, when the cock crows thrice. A gloom compounded with dread descends immediately upon the company. Crick's wife hastily glosses over this ominous incident, but the air of foreboding is only enhanced (*Tess of the d'Urbervilles* 213). Their fears are proved true when, a little later, Retty Priddle is reported to have tried to drown herself from a broken heart (218–19).

Tennant recognises the value of this episode for her intertextual purposes and re-casts it within a metafictional context. In *Tess,* a dramatic version of *Tess of the d'Urbervilles*, in which Thomas Hardy is a principal actor, is scheduled, and during the rehearsal, a cock happens to crow, anticipating the play. The excerpt is as follows:

> A cock crows.
>
> This kind of thing is always happening to Thomas Hardy. What he writes take place—years later, sometimes, but recognizably from one of his books—and people regard him with some fear and awe, some hostility, as a man uncomfortably close to the supernatural.
>
> (Tennant 159)

The rehearsal goes on, and then, true to Hardy's text, news reaches them a while later that a girl has drowned herself at Chesil Beach. Tennant's inclusion of this feature from Hardy's plot, as well as her manner of including it, has several implications, such as:

a) At the most basic level, it redirects the reader to Hardy's *Tess of the d'Urbervilles* and operates as a straightforward vehicle of intertextuality.

b) It concurrently confirms the generic affinity between *Tess* and the ballad, by bringing a typical feature of the ballad within the purview of the novel.

c) It implicitly raises questions about the causal connection between life and art. Does the former inspire the latter, or is a counter-inspiration also possible? This metafictional question is underscored by the observation about Hardy that 'what he writes takes place'. This remark suggests that Hardy's texts predestine real life.

Intertextual Sites

Tennant's compulsion to repeat the 'Tess' ballad is ideologically motivated by the fact that patriarchal narratives have done no justice to the depiction of Tess. By giving the story a balladic structure, she hints that it is a universal and recurring one, besides dating earlier than Hardy's written version. Traditionally, the ballad-singer distanced himself from an emotional involvement in his story; but Hardy's narration is hardly impersonal. In her version Tennant stakes her claim that Hardy is non-feminist and supports it with facts from his life. He caused other 'Tess' stories to happen, such as those of Augusta Way and Gertrude Bugler, who paid the price of being admired by Hardy.

To highlight her novel's intertextual status, Tennant resorts to a formal device that is more striking than the ballad features hitherto employed. Inverted commas are commonly used not only for conveying direct speech, but also to suggest a different and intrusive text (as in the case of quotations). They are thus glaring intertextual devices. Tennant's adoption of the ballad is based on a tacit acceptance that the reader is listening (rather than reading) to Liza-Lu's 'song'; by this token, the entire narration (novel) should be framed by inverted commas. By the same logic, conversational excerpts within the narrative need not be marked. However, Tennant does neither of the above. Inverted commas in *Tess* are used self-consciously, only while referring to Hardy's novel. To take an instance, Tennant quotes passages from *Tess of the d'Urbervilles* which variously describe Tess's mouth (Tennant 57, *Tess of the d'Urbervilles* 8, 9, 49, 89, 148, 166). These inverted commas primarily alert the reader into observing the juxtapositioning of two texts, as a result of the entry of *Tess of the d'Urbervilles* into *Tess.* Thus Liza-Lu's remarks to Ella, although conversational, forego the markers, since Tennant sees them as part of one textual segment, which is *her Tess*. All dialogues that come in the sphere of the twentieth-century version of *Tess* are by-passed without these signifiers.

Hardy becomes an intertextual presence in *Tess* for two reasons. One is on account of his novel, *Tess of the d'Urbervilles.* The other is constituted by details from his personal life; Tennant intersperses these in her intertextual allusions in such a way that they become relevant to her feminist mission.

The Ballad as Text

It is quite possible that Tennant derived the balladic identity of the Tess-story from a sentence in *Tess of the d'Urbervilles.* After being seduced by Alec, Tess returns to Marlott and helps in the harvesting to make herself useful. Here 'Tess's female companions sang songs, and showed themselves very sympathetic and glad at her reappearance out of doors, though they could not refrain from mischievously throwing in a few verses of the ballad about the maid who went to the merry green wood and came back a changed state' (*Tess of the d'Urbervilles* 90).

As Tennant has a feminist mission, she advances the idea of the interchangeability of the ballad and history, also indicating thereby that for women, who were storytellers before the era of the written record, the ballad was their version of history. The ballad is also *their* history.

Therefore the Liza-Lu of *Tess,* who insists on calling her ballad 'history' in flagrant disregard of Ella's dislike of the term, is not making a mistake. Ella abhors the history taught in school because it consists of 'the succession of lifeless kings and stale-smelling politicians' (Tennant 5). But Liza-Lu has a reason for merging the identity of the two discourses. For her the only history that matters is the Tess–story, since it serves as a cautionary tale for future generations of women. Therefore it is important for Ella to learn this lesson 'of the Then, the Here and the Now' (Tennant 5) even if at the expense of school lessons. Although the principal listener, Baby Tess, is a veritable infant, the point of this ballad is that a female can never be too young to internalise this moral.

The ballad shares the medieval aura of the romance, and likewise, is not typically Victorian. It is typical, if at all, of pre-writing, just as the Tess–story too is pre-Victorian. Folklore and myth play a major role in its composition and transmission; while its history is so ancient that it dates from the Celts themselves. The question that comes to mind now is: from where does Tennant derive the Victorian identity of the ballad?

The answer is, from Hardy's version of the ballad, *Tess of the d'Urbervilles*, which is periodically recalled by Tennant. The Victorian reference is thus established. Meanwhile, to Liza-Lu goes the credit of bestowing a postmodern flavour to *Tess*. Despite being a marginal character in both novels, she is apportioned the all-important role of narration. Her relatively insignificant role in the story enables her to merge her individual experience as a woman within the collective female experiences of suffering as well as storytelling.

The changes in Tennant's version are of considerable significance. Hardy's Tess gives birth to a boy who dies a few days later. Tennant's Tess has a daughter, and she in turn has a daughter. Unlike Hardy, moreover, who abandons Tess to the judgement of the 'President of the Immortals' (*Tess of the d'Urbervilles* 390), Tennant endows her Tess with resilience and retains hope for the future, almost in the face of all odds. The only hope for the Tesses of the world lies in narration, the age-old profession of women. When Liza-Lu insists on telling baby Tess the story, she is not only fulfilling a natural vocation, but also attempting thereby to break the vicious cycle of love, betrayal, revenge and murder.

THE FAIRY TALE

There are two major fairy tales in *Possession*, both of which are authored by Christabel LaMotte, the Victorian heroine of *Possession.* Their nested position inside a novelistic narrative endows them with the status of intertextual devices. Byatt thereafter stretches their intertextual range to include other voices, such as the feminist text in the case of 'The Glass Coffin'. In the chapter, 'Gender and Intertextuality' we shall examine this fairy tale for its overt feminist bearings.

Several generic features of the fairy tale such as fantastic adventures, talking animals, magical gifts, metamorphoses, condition-bound offers and choices to the characters, all make their presence in 'The Glass Coffin'. Ostensibly a children's story, this is actually a problematic text that begins to deconstruct itself right at the beginning. A little later the narrator describes the tailor as going through the forest 'in search of work *perhaps*' (*Possession* 58, emphasis mine), as if she does not indeed know. This remark is very unlike an omniscient narrator, and besides it also jeopardises narrative authority. At another juncture in the narrative, a gesture is made towards textuality by alluding to generic regulations: 'And he knew—*it is always so, after all*—that the true adventure was the release of this sleeper, who would then be his grateful bride' (*Possession* 63, emphasis mine). The predetermined narrative grammar of fairy tales is self-reflexively evoked in sentences such as this, making their author Christabel a postmodern writer.

Intertextuality is overlaid with self-reflexivity in 'The Glass Coffin'. Christabel is well aware of the incongruities and absurdities demanded by the genre of the fairy tale, and cannot – or will not – keep the knowledge hidden in the narrative. Another instance is her narration of the tailor's rescue of the young damsel. When he opens her coffin with his key, the sleeping lady opens her eyes, and the little tailor, *because he knew this was what he must do*, bent and kissed the perfect cheek' (*Possession* 63, emphasis mine). This phrase with which the narrator intrudes into the story, conveys the idea that the tailor is obeying a textual convention rather than an impulse in kissing the beautiful woman. Simultaneously there is an advertisement of textuality in the way in which the genre imposes its disciplinary procedures on the characters inhabiting its world.

The tailor's compliance with the self-questioning intentions of the text is almost innocent; as for example, when the time comes for him to accept the damsel in marriage. 'Of course I will have you,' he says, 'Though why you should have me, simply because I opened the glass case, is less clear to me altogether. . .' (*Possession* 66). He does not undergo any promotion in status that would make him an eligible suitor to the damsel, and remains the 'little' tailor to the very end (*Possession* 67). It is possible, then, to see 'The Glass Coffin' as a perverse rewriting of such famous stories as 'Sleeping Beauty'.

If the tailor-hero's absence of ardour is unnatural in a fairy tale, there is an equally unnatural intimacy between the damsel and her brother. Indeed, the only affectionate exchange in this story is between them: 'And they embraced, for a long time, with full hearts' (*Possession* 67). Despite sharing a home with the rescued lady the tailor remains outside her sphere and here we have a strange case of 'living happily ever after'. 'The young man and his sister went hunting in the wild woods, and the little tailor, whose inclination did not lie that way, stayed by the hearth and was merry with them in the evenings' (*Possession* 67).

Fissures in the fairy-tale fabric such as these obtrude themselves with intertextual intent, giving the lie to token beginnings and endings as 'There was once a little tailor. . .' (*Possession* 58) and 'And so it was, and they did live happily ever after' (*Possession* 67) respectively.

The second fairy tale written by Christabel, 'The Threshold', is also characterised by textual gaps that accommodate self-reflexivity. This is a tale of quest by a Childe, and has points of similarity with 'The Glass Coffin'. Like the three gifts from which the tailor has to choose in the latter story, the Childe has to select one of three beautiful women as his guide. The Childe conforms to the stipulations of the genre by choosing the third and least alluring lady. Christabel comments on the proceeding in a highly self-conscious manner: 'And you know, and I know, do we not, dear children, that he must always choose this last, and the leaden casket, for wisdom in all tales tells us this, and the last sister is always the true choice, is she not?' (*Possession* 155).

Here as well as periodically in the story, Christabel turns the mirror from the world of reality to the text itself. Sentences therefore break in self-consciously, 'Such is the power of necessity in tales' (*Possession* 155). These breaks urge the reader to come out of the world of the text and recognise it as a representation. In fact the title 'The Threshold' suggests boundaries, which are crucial for intertextuality to come into its own. For an intertextual pattern is produced not merely by textual plurality, but by the identification of plurality, which is made possible by margins that demarcate individual texts. Margins can reveal themselves in several ways: novels like *Possession* and *FLW* rely on changes in print to highlight them. Byatt makes a leitmotif of the threshold metaphor through the novel; it emerges again and again, whether in the plural voices of the dramatic monologue, or in a title like 'The Shadowy Portal'.

The threshold has a metaphoric function in the fairy tale under discussion. The gateway becomes a literal marker between the known and the unknown, which the Childe has to step over. Other kinds of thresholds also make themselves visible to an imaginative reader, such as the ontological threshold between illusion (the world of the imagination) and reality.

In the first stage of his quest, the Childe comes upon a passage. 'At the end of the avenue was a building, or structure, with huge gateposts and a heavy roofing stone and a stone to mark a threshold' (*Possession* 151). Beyond this is the growing dark out of which step three beautiful women, each with her own attraction for the Childe. He meets the ladies appropriately enough at twilight, which may be termed threshold-time. After the Childe chooses the third lady his adventure intensifies into an experience of the frontier as he follows his chosen guide. She draws him down a road bathed in the glow of the dusk, 'lit by a light neither of day nor of night, neither of sun nor of moon, neither light nor shadowy, but the even perpetual unchanging light of that kingdom. . .' (*Possession* 156). The reader tempted to linger in this poetically sensitive evocation of threshold is in for a disappointment, as the author's signature 'Christabel LaMotte', interrupts the reverie to signal the border between the levels of illusion and reality.

Christabel seems to delight in such thresholds. Pretending an inability to describe the beautiful eyes of the maiden, she creates another threshold to come out of the narrative and address the reader: 'If I were to attempt this description—but no, I cannot—yet I must, for I am your chronicler, bound to recount to you, what?' (*Possession* 155).

THE ROMANCE

A major hurdle in the way of defining the romance is the difficulty of a precise definition for the term. The frequency and looseness of the term contribute considerably to its diffuseness. To give a simplistic example, unlike specialised and rigidly structured literary genres like the ode or the sonnet, the 'romance' is semantically interchangeable with 'love', and thus invested with connotative baggage.

According to Schmidt and Jacobs, romances are 'stories in verse which deal with the adventures of noble men and women and which end happily'. The authors concede that the definition is 'vague', but 'it goes as far as the evidence permits'(Schmidt and Jacobs 1).

Broadly speaking, romances have all or most of the following features. They tell a narrative of love and chivalric adventure; they have a setting that is temporally and geographically remote; there is an atmosphere of the marvellous and fantastic as a corollary to its remoteness of setting; there is idealism; and all of these are invested with the object of recreational entertainment. This freedom in the outlines of romance encourages its boundary-crossing into the neighbouring generic domains of the ballad and the epic. It is easier in fact to define the romance in contradistinctive terms, by comparing it with a novel or even history, which are realistic modes.

Atmosphere or ambience plays a pervasive role in romances; recognising this, Byatt liberally endows *Possession* with it. Being widespread and general, the romance stands in danger of being cast aside as a generic characteristic rather than a genre. It is to Byatt's credit that she makes as effective an intertextual vehicle of the romance as she does of the dramatic monologue. Unlike the romance, the latter is typified by a clarity and precision of form which makes its representation comparatively easier. Through the diary of Sabine de Kercoz Byatt shows the romance to be truly intertextual by showing its potential for self-reflexivity. We shall look at this aspect after a general assessment of the genre.

Besides the characteristics that are peculiar to itself as a genre, the romance also engenders a particular attitude, especially from among élitist readers. This is largely one of condescension. Attitude is an important dimension of intertextuality, a point we have made clear in the discussion on echoic utterances. Byatt appears to acknowledge this, as *Possession* is a valiant attempt to revise the attitude of condescension that a romance generally provokes. Condescension towards the romance is a tendency as old as the Greeks themselves; a more familiar and less remote example offers itself with *Don Quixote* (1612–20).

There were occasional exceptions, of course. By the end of the eighteenth and the beginning of the nineteenth centuries, 'romance' had come to signify 'flights of fancy and imagination' (Cuddon 580). This period ushered in the Romantic Movement, and for a while a change of heart ensued *vis-à-vis* the romance. The Romantic Revival revised the hitherto downgraded status of the romance, by glamorising it with enchantment born of an atmosphere compounded in the main of medievalism. Keats's poem, 'The Eve of St. Agnes', is a case in point and another example is Coleridge's 'Christabel'. The latter is important for the purposes of this chapter as it determines the textuality of *Possession* to a large extent.

Romance / 'A' Romance

Byatt's use of an article before 'romance', in the subtitle to her novel, may be glossed by the following observation: 'From the Romantic period onwards writers more and more abandon the article before "romance". Romance has become a literary quality rather than a form and it is frequently set against "reality" in literary argument' (Gillian Beer, *The Romance* 66). The genre that claims to represent 'reality' is the novel, and Hawthorne measures the romance against the novel in his famous preface to *The House of the Seven Gables* (1).

The subtitle of Byatt's novel is 'A Romance'. Subtitles are common enough in Victorian novels; 'A Novel without a Hero' (*Vanity Fair*) or 'A Pure Woman' (*Tess of the d'Urbervilles*) are two popular examples. When Byatt uses this convention she furthers the Victorianist dynamics of her novel by rejecting a subtitle that would address the novel's mimetic world, and instead choosing a phrase that defines the generic identity of *Possession.* In short, a subtitle such as 'A Pure Woman' is a direct pointer to the theme of *Tess of the d'Urbervilles*. But 'A Romance' alerts the reader to the textual conventions of *Possession* rather than its theme or story.

The Romance and the Novel

Byatt's subtitle also brings into focus the uneasy relationship between the novel and the romance. This uneasiness dates back to *Don Quixote*, the first ever novel, which came into being by parodying the conventions of the romance. The knowledge that the romance had an identifiable set of features that lend themselves to imitation – and mockery as well – makes this genre a potential vehicle of self-reflexivity, which Byatt exploits in *Possession*.

Since the romance is anti-novel in its assumptions of non-verisimilitude in representation, Byatt may also be raising fundamental questions about the form of her own novel; in her subtitle lie embedded the following queries: is this a novel or a romance? There is an alternative question: is this a novel that is *also* a romance? The tension generated by the conflicting directions of these two questions contributes to the postmodern temper of *Possession*. Moreover, to call a sophisticated text such as *Possession* 'A Romance', seems both provocative and ironical when one recalls such canonical novels as *Northanger Abbey* and *Madame Bovary,* that invoke the conventions and assumptions of the romance only to subvert them.

Byatt's mission with the romance is indeed provocative. She attempts to reinstate it into the canon; through *Possession* she tries to centre the marginal role it has played *vis-à-vis* the novel, in a typical postmodern exercise. Irony helps Byatt because it complicates the message of the subtitle: '[Both] irony [and parody] may be said to confuse the normal processes of communication by offering more than one message to be decoded by the reader. . .' (Rose 87).

Reviewing the history of the genre of the romance in England, Beer distinguishes two watersheds: 'they both have to do with an increasing *self-consciousness* about the way the form is used' (*The Romance* 6, emphasis mine). The first, *Don Quixote*, satirically revised the romance and accelerated its downward shift within literary hierarchy, by fostering an ironic perspective. The second, the romantic revival, revered the world of romance. So if one were to look for precursors to the attitude of *Possession* to the romance, one would have to locate them in the second watershed. *Possession* aligns itself with the second perspective, but validates it in its own unique way. It does this (as already pointed out) by investing the romance with the potential for self-reflexivity.

Possession

Gillian Beer maintains that the primary objective of the romance is to entertain, however lofty be its literary and moral qualities (*The Romance* 3). Even while obeying this dictum, *Possession* goes ahead of this limited demand made of it. Like the dramatic monologue, the other genre that determines the plot of *Possession*, the romance too belongs both to the Victorians as well as the postmoderns. There is, however, one difference. The dramatic monologue is an obvious genre to indicate the Victorians, where Browning is neatly substituted by Ash. The romance, on the other hand, is a difficult proposition, as it does not suggest the Victorian period in the way the genres of the dramatic monologue or the novel do. The romance is in fact the genre of the middle ages[3].

Nevertheless, the ancient lineage and protean spirit of the romance encourage the essentially postmodern exercise of re-employing literature of the past. Byatt's self-reflexive use of the romance in *Possession* endows it with a metafictional role that draws it into the domain of postmodernism. It may be useful to ask why Byatt uses Hawthorne's definition of the romance as an epigraph, rather than incorporate it textually. The latter could easily have been achieved, since *Possession* is peopled with literary critics and English academics. But it is only by retaining it as a text distinct from the main novel, that the reader can be prompted to see the novel as an illustration of the principles of the romance–genre. The definition from Hawthorne's Preface to *The House of the Seven Gables* is as follows. 'The point of view in which this tale comes under the Romantic definition lies in the attempt to connect a bygone time with the very present that is flitting away from us'. (Hawthorne 1, quoted in *Possession*).

Possession does 'attempt to connect a bygone time with the very present that is flitting away from us', both in its narrative as well as in its interactive generic structure. Not only are there are at least two major love affairs in *Possession*, one Victorian, and the other set in the twentieth century, the romance of Ash and Christabel also has an allegorical extension. Allegory is one of the commonest modes of producing meaning in the romance. Christabel's surname LaMotte, is French for 'the word', and by extension Ash's love affair comes to be read as an extremely enriching and productive liaison with words. A symbolic interpretation of Christabel's name is suggested by Ash himself. Struck by the intertextual associations of her name, he writes to Christabel, 'I was emboldened by your mention of the Ancient Mariner to wonder – was it *he* who named you and was that for Coleridge's heroine of his unfinished poem?' (*Possession* 175).

Byatt maximises this intertextual connection by investing it with the prominent landmarks of romance. These are features enumerated by Beer as natural to nineteenth-century romances and chief among them are allegory, horror and psychological fantasy.

Mystery, allegory and sexuality are the prime ingredients constituting the imaginative world of Coleridge's poem, 'Christabel' as well as the fictional life of Byatt's heroine, Christabel. In Byatt's schema Christabel LaMotte is a 'real' character, named after a poem by Coleridge. Assuming this to be provisionally true within the world of the narrative, it follows that a real-life character, Christabel, is not just named after a character in a book but also partakes of the character of the persona she is named after. Life thus becomes subject to the influence of a text. The normal direction of 'life → inspiring → text' is reversed in this new equation that Byatt formulates. This indeed takes fictional self-consciousness to a metaphysical extreme.

Byatt's intertextual play with names and their possibilities is no doubt advantaged by the incompleteness of Coleridge's text. Textual incompleteness is an active incentive for intertextuality. Coleridge's unfinished poem goads Ash to react strongly, 'I cannot bear not to know the end of a tale. . .' (*Possession* 176). It annoys him that the secret of Coleridge's 'Christabel' 'sleeps with its lethargic and inconsequential author—who cares not for our irritable quandary' (*Possession* 176). Taking cognisance of her character's complaint, Byatt herself is careful to withhold none of her Christabel's secrets from the reader, and even adds a postscript to reveal the whole truth. In an interesting move, the genre that reveals the mystery of Christabel's whereabouts during her pregnancy is the romance, which is found, of all places, inside the journal of Sabine de Kercoz.

The central narrative segment of the heroine in both tales, Christabel in 'Christabel' and Christabel in *Possession*, consists of her sexual awakening. Amour is the soul of romance: to which a dash of piquancy is added by hinting that the heroine in each case has a lesbian experience. In Coleridge's romance, an enchantress called Geraldine seduces the innocent Christabel into sin (*sic* - Coleridge's moral judgement cannot escape the reader's notice). Then, through magic, Geraldine exercises her power and imposes silence on Christabel. Similarly in *Possession* too, a sexual relationship between Blanche and Christabel is suggested more than once.

While in 'Christabel' Geraldine appropriates the power of speech all to herself, in *Possession* other generic voices prevent the hegemony of a single voice of authority. Letters between Ash and Christabel, the diaries of Blanche, Ellen and Sabine, and the omniscient narrator's text interact with each other to create a more democratic text. The courtly world of romance with its monarchic spirit is defeated by the postmodern world that espouses egalitarianism. When Coleridge's Geraldine claims sole authority to speak 'the truth', she behaves like the speaker of a dramatic monologue. Since the latter is also a powerful text in this novel, the romance and the dramatic monologue briefly meet in their ideological position towards narratorial hegemony. Though they are mutually supportive in rendering this Victorian novel as Victorianist, their respective textual shapes are mutually exclusive, in this case; the monologue has a form which is determined and closely structured, while Ariel-like, the romance enjoys sporting a wide variety of shapes.

Another ingredient is the quest-motif that plays an important role in romance-narratives. The central quest in *Possession* is a manuscript-hunt. Roland's interest in the Victorian love-story of Ash and Christabel is aroused by Ash's letter, which he reads in the library, and this becomes the starting-point of *Possession*. In all the stages of this quest, a text plays a prominent role. Ash's letter to Christabel functions as a *billet-doux* that leads Roland and Maud to other texts, such as the correspondence between Ash and Christabel, or Sabine de Kercoz's diary. It is noteworthy that a romantic story is woven into each of these texts. The text-hunt in turn becomes responsible for the love that blossoms between Roland and Maud. This 'search–discovery' paradigm is endowed with much excitement and suspense in *Possession*.

The Romance in *Possession*

In the nineteenth-century plot-strand of *Possession*, Christabel LaMotte occupies the status of a major writer of romances. Christabel's most famous literary work is her metrical romance *Melusina*. Though bearing the nomenclature of 'epic' within the covers of *Possession* (36), it gives proof of a quicksilver generic character that is natural to a romance. It reinforces its inherent intertextuality in other ways as well; Gillian Beer, for instance, specifies 'Melusine' as a romance of the fourteenth century (*The Romance* 24) and Christabel's poem may safely be assumed as the continuation of a tradition. This kind of interfacing between fictional and historically 'real' writing is a tool familiar to intertextuality. The 'real' 'Melusina', compiled by Jean d'Arras, is a *chanson de geste*, which is a poem that relates heroic deeds, and usually combines history and legend (Cuddon 109). *Melusina* affirms that it is a romance in several of its basic traits. Book 1 of this poem sets the scene for a sexual encounter between the adventuring Knight Raimondin, and the beautiful, self-possessed lady he meets: 'Now was he hers, if she should ask of him/ Body or soul, he would have offered all' (*Possession* 298). Raimondin's infatuation recalls Keats's literary ballad, 'La Belle Dame sans Merci". More powerfully, it recalls an unmistakable convention of romance exhibited in the tradition of courtly love where the male pays homage to his lady-love.

There is some degree of overlap between the features of the romance and the epic, which could blunt the inter-generic boundary-crossing procedures. But when the romance is interfaced with the novel, intertextuality becomes a sharply visible activity. The reader who is tuned into the novelistic mode of vraisemblance (the French equivalent of 'verisimilitude' which means 'having the appearance of truth'. This quality is achieved in literature through a skilful selection, ordering and presentation of human life) is startled to encounter elements of the marvellous and fantastic in his text. Whereas with genres like the ballad and the epic, the romance enjoys an affinity that makes intertextuality a subtler happening. Common generic features blur individual silhouettes so that the reader can mistake one for the other.

Sabine de Kercoz's journal is the text where Byatt locates the romance in its most appealing form. Sabine's journal reinforces the French connection of the genre, by being written by a Frenchwoman who lives in Brittany. The 'French' ambience of the romance was a product of social influences, chief among these being the Norman conquest of England in 1066 AD. English romances of the middle ages were heavily dependent upon French counterparts, and the latter served as models for the former (Burrow 8).

The diary of Sabine de Kercoz, recording the arrival of Christabel for her confinement, forcefully locates the romance in a forty-four-page-long text (*Possession* 335–79). The 'character' of this memoir is very different from Ellen's, which is the other journal in *Possession*.

Kercoz's journal is fundamentally a disquisition on literature and literary conventions.

The setting of these journal entries is Brittany, a place especially conducive to the nurturing of romance. Of the place Sabine declares: 'In this misty land the borderline between myth, legend and fact is not decisive, my father says, as a stone arch might be between this world and another, but more like a series of moving veils or woven webs between one room and another' (*Possession* 339). Here we have Hawthorne's twilight land of the romance, where the worlds of reality and illusion walk effortlessly into each other, enacting a metafictional principle. 'In Brittany', says Sabine, 'a man could fall down a well and find himself in a summer land of apples' (*Possession* 364). Brittany also has its very own story-teller in the father of Sabine. Raoul de Kercoz is steeped in the mythology of the land and is an expert raconteur: 'Every winter, he tells the tale of Merlin and Vivien, always the same tale, never twice the same telling' (*Possession* 353). This sentence also illustrates the principle of intertextuality in its underlying assumption of the re-usable imagination and variable echoes.

The self-reflexive slot that the romance occupies in Byatt's scheme is emphasised at the outset of this journal, which is simultaneously a female writer's attempt at writing and her expression of the travails of writing. Sabine also comments on genres; here Byatt reverses accepted norms by having Sabine repudiate received notions of the romance as 'the repetitious vapours and ecstatic sighing of commonplace girls with commonplace feelings' (*Possession* 340). 'The pleasures of writing are various. The language of reflection has its own pleasure and the language of narration quite a different one', writes Sabine in an entry (*Possession* 344). Sabine's journal not only questions the patriarchal hegemony of writing, but also shows an alternate mode of storytelling, typical of the romance, one which comes naturally to women such as Gode.

Sabine's journal moreover places the romance in the form of an inset story told by Gode, who is a living embodiment of the world of the romance. Gode finds the spirit-world with its implausible happenings, and the mundane world of logic and reason equally acceptable. One world is no less real than the other, even though both are mutually exclusive. Gode's way of accounting for it is through the concept of 'threshold'. She tells tales of the Baie des Trepasses, which is 'not so much the Bay of the Dead as the bay of those who have crossed the barrier which divides this world from *that*. . . where two worlds cross' (*Possession* 355). Similarly real life and the world of texts are believed to be compatible, and traffic between them becomes two-way.

Gode's story is about a sailor and his rejected lady-love. She has a child out of wedlock whom she murders, and which thereafter haunts her as a spirit. Her faithless sailor-lover does return to her after a lapse of time, but it is too late, as she is under the spell of the mysterious feet (presumably of the murdered child that she cannot see but only hear) that drive her to madness and suicide. Meanwhile the sailor marries another woman called Jeanne, but his respite is short-lived. The feet come back to haunt him and he too is driven to death.

This story is replete with most of the features of the romance such as love, supernatural elements, and mystery. Its site is also noteworthy, in that it is twice-embedded: it is framed by Sabine's journal, which in turn is enclosed in the larger narrative of *Possession*. While *Possession* has other embedded texts as well, such as *Melusina*, the dramatic monologue 'Mummy Possest' or Ellen Ash's journal, the romance is embedded twice, thus re-asserting its self-examining status.

The tension between the power of the romance to enslave and charm, and the intertextual artillery to break the state of enchantment induced by the romance, contributes greatly to the appeal of *Possession*. In daring to break natural laws and explore other dimensions, the romance becomes a paradigm for wish-fulfilment. By extension it also becomes a paradigm for the Victorianist desire to remake the Victorians in our image.

NOTES

1 The enlarged characters intimate the beginning of a new chapter in Tennant's *Tess* (London: Harper Collins, 1993) 9.

2 The verb 'survive' has been used here because intertextual borrowing, particularly where mystery is woven into the plot, has to be judicious. For instance, if the point of the earlier work is the unravelling of the mystery, then the latter work must go a step ahead and ensure that suspense, which is integral for sustaining that mystery, is not destroyed.

3 Medieval literature enjoyed a revival in the poetic works of Tennyson (who reworked the Arthurian legends of Sir Thomas Malory) and the Pre-Raphaelite poets. Romance, it seems, was already an intertextual genre for the Victorians.

3 The Novel

The Victorianist novels come into being in flagrant defiance of a prevalent suspicion regarding the novel: that it is dead[1]. They affirm that it still exists, and then reaffirm it. They verify it by taking recourse to the great Victorian novels of Dickens, Hardy, George Eliot and the Brontës for inspiration; and again confirm it by perpetuating these *ur*-texts in the same generic mode, the novel. It is part of the Victorianist intertextual exercise to protract the novel form, especially in the light of Bakhtin's claim that it was the leading European genre of the second half of the nineteenth century (*The Dialogic Imagination* 41).

> What was gradually achieved in the nineteenth-century novel is analogous with what happened in the gradual evolution of Elizabethan drama, most conspicuously in Shakespeare's and Ben Jonson's work. A loose assemblage of episodes, lacking any strongly focussed intention, gradually gave place to those powerful visions of human life which we have in, for example *Macbeth* and *Volpone*. (Klingopulos 101)

It is a transformation that one can identify, for instance, in the career of a representative Victorian novelist like Dickens, which begins with the picaresque *The Pickwick Papers* (1836–37) and matures in an artistic *tour de force* such as *Great Expectations* (1860–61).

The Victorian age saw a host of brilliant novelists creating their own version of the novel. The spectrum ranges from Thackeray's satirical novel of manners, *Vanity Fair* (1848), to Emily Brontë's unrestrained narrative of passion, *Wuthering Heights* (1847). Certain conventions were nevertheless taken for granted, such as a structurally coherent plot, and an unambiguous notion of character. Both these ideas are subverted by the postmodern generation of novelists. Indeed when the novel moved into the late twentieth century after the ravages of the modernist and postmodernist movements, it seemed to have little, if anything, in common with its Victorian ancestor. Most noteworthy is the presence of self-consciousness or metafiction in the Victorianist novel (as a result of postmodernist influence), which enables the Victorianist novel to be 'different' from the Victorian novel, and belong to the category of intertextual rather than historical fiction.

A Non-Victorianist Intertextual Narrative to Explain Intertextuality

Let us now see how a work written in the twentieth century can become intertextual with the Victorian novel, by incorporating self-consciousness. Jorge Luis Borges' short story, 'Pierre Menard, Author of the *Quixote*' (*Labyrinths* 62–71) is a disquisition on the efforts of Menard, the protagonist, to rewrite *Don Quixote* word for word. Menard, it is stressed, is not copying from the original; he is writing *Don Quixote* all over again. Menard's enterprise implicitly raises anew the debate over originality and imitation. One of the things it does is to challenge the received notion of the former as superior to the latter, by confusing the boundary between the two. In fact Menard's work is intertextuality of the highest order, where the inter-referencing is so acute as to result in a facsimile replica. A seeming contradiction concerning imitation *vis-à-vis* intertextuality is herein raised; that while on the face of it, intertextuality depends on a recognisable imitation, it is an inspired imitation that has nothing to do with replication.

The effort that goes into the making of an intertextual work, and the high premium on creativity that such an undertaking imposes, is brought home to the reader quite categorically by the narrator of 'Pierre Menard'. 'He did not want to compose another *Quixote* - which is easy - but the *Quixote* itself. Needless to say, he never contemplated mechanical transcription of the original' (*Labyrinths* 65). This is a pointer to the paradox that intertextuality precariously balances itself upon creativity not despite, but due to, imitation.

This illustration is perhaps an approach to the Victorianist novel by indirection, but it is a useful digression. One can fruitfully compare the following statements with the relationship of the Victorianist to the Victorian novel: 'To compose the *Quixote* at the beginning of the seventeenth century was a reasonable undertaking, necessary and perhaps even unavoidable; at the beginning of the twentieth, it is almost impossible. It is not in vain that three hundred years have gone by, filled with exceedingly complex events. Among them, to mention only one, is the *Quixote* itself' (*Labyrinths* 68).

Compare this with a Victorianist novel like John Fowles's *FLW*. Fowles claims that it is the Victorian novel *par excellence* that the Victorians failed to write. His claim is not to be read naïvely or literally; Fowles is referring to the impossibility of writing like a Victorian in the late twentieth century. His observation brings him close to Menard's discovery that in the centuries following the writing of the *Quixote*, the *Quixote* itself is an important landmark to be reckoned with, and hence the *Quixote* cannot be written now. Similarly, the Victorianists cannot write like the Victorians, because the latter have become a part of the decades leading to the Victorianists, who have to take this fact into their reckoning.

Encountering an intertextual novel is thus fraught with excitement for the discerning reader. 'Menard... has enriched, by means of a new technique, the halting and rudimentary art of reading: this new technique is that of the deliberate anachronism and the erroneous attribution... This technique fills the most placid works with adventure' (*Labyrinths* 71). Here is at least one justification for intertextuality, if it needs any: Victorianist fiction revitalises literature, particularly at a time when the funereal dirge for the novel seems to have sounded.

The Novel and Intrinsic Intertextuality

In its postmodern existence, the novel has come to stay as the most suitable vehicle of intertextuality. For being perceived in this new avatar, it is beholden to M. M. Bakhtin who played a major role in laying bare the polyphonic nature of this genre. Bakhtin comes to the crux of the matter when he comments on the total inadequacy of literary theory in describing the novel (*The Dialogic Imagination* 8). He attributes this to the relatively fluid generic state of the novel, which, unlike most other genres, resists straitjacketing. In the Bakhtinian mode of perception, this is a strength rather than a handicap, as it enables the novel to be intertextual.

The novel is quintessentially an 'inclusive' genre and 'is characterised (we need only recall Rabelais and Cervantes) precisely by its tendency to embrace other genres, to absorb philosophical and scientific knowledge' (Kundera 64). The novel is an open-ended form (*The Dialogic Imagination* 7) which makes it a convenient vehicle for intertextuality.

The most obvious kind of intertextuality that the Victorianist novel indulges in, is textual juxtaposition, 'text' in this context being synonymous with 'genre'. A good illustration is *Possession*, wherein a foreign genre like the dramatic monologue is comfortably entrenched within the novelistic narrative. Moreover, the inclusion of the dramatic monologue does not make *Possession* any less a novel. Bakhtin sees this kind of accommodation as characteristic of the novel right from its beginnings. From its incipience to the later stages of its development, 'the novel makes wide and substantial use of letters, diaries, confessions, the forms and methods of rhetoric associated with recently established courts and so forth' (*The Dialogic Imagination* 33). Its leaning is towards generic variety, a fact fully absorbed by the Victorianist novels of this study.

The novel can incorporate other genres in itself, and fare none the worse for it; 'The image of another's language and outlook on the world. . . simultaneously represented *and* representing, is extremely typical of the novel' (*The Dialogic Imagination* 45). Dialogism between the novelistic and other textual forms grants the novel its singular status as an embedding genre. Discussing the underlying potential of the novel for overt intertextuality, Bakhtin claims, 'One of the most basic and fundamental forms for incorporating and organizing heteroglossia[2] in the novel' is that of 'incorporated genres' (*The Dialogic Imagination* 320).

Bakhtin establishes the uniqueness of the novel by differentiating it from other genres like poetry and drama. Poetry as understood in the sense of verse, has an established poetics, and so does drama; whereas the novel stands in need of a theoretical context as well as respectability in literary circles. Being intrinsically heteroglot, unlike poetic genres which are monologic and unilateral, the novel is a complex structure (*The Dialogic Imagination* 284). An intertextual novel is the most 'novel'-like of the various types and captures the essence of the genre by accentuating its multi-generic personality[3].

Effortlessly dialogic, the novel easily gives space for more than one mode of representing life. Its perception of life is centripetal rather than centrifugal. The poet's world, on the other hand, is centrifugal; and a poem uses words 'without mediation' and 'without quotation marks' (*The Dialogic Imagination* 285). Even drama, it appears, is not dialogic, despite the fact that the dialogue is a dramatic convention. 'Pure drama strives toward a unitary language. . . Dramatic dialogue is determined by a collision between individuals who exist within the limits of a single world and a single unitary language' (*The Dialogic Imagination* 405).

The novel also comes closest to everyday language. Bakhtin validates this assertion by citing intertextuality to be a phenomenon that is ever present in social interaction. In everyday language, one is always referring to somebody else's speech or opinion; sometimes one acknowledges the source; at other times one plagiarises. Here Bakhtin stresses the importance of attitude and how it can alter meaning. 'The context embracing another's word is responsible for its dialogizing background, whose influence can be very great. Given the appropriate methods for framing, one may bring about fundamental changes even in another's utterance accurately quoted' (*The Dialogic Imagination* 340).

To the question, how the Victorian is re-styled as Victorianist, the answer comes from Bakhtin: 'The novelistic discourse dominating a given epoch is itself turned into an object and itself becomes a means for refracting new authorial intentions' (*The Dialogic Imagination* 309).

The Victorians who are the representing agents in one historical period, succumb to the exigencies of time, and a hundred years later they become the 'represented'. In the new context, their conventions of representation undergo an altered mode of perception and the re-deployment of the very same conventions now becomes overlaid with other contemporary echoes. Let us take just one convention, that of the omniscient narrator; Fowles shows that in the twentieth century the concept of the omniscient and omnipotent narrator is suspect, and repudiates the Victorian convention of the all-powerful God in the theory and practice of *FLW*.

Bakhtin introduces the concept of re-accentuation to explain the role played by context in altering ways and methods of perceiving old conventions. The notion of re-accentuation also helps to emphasise the difference between the Victorianist and the historical novel. 'Every age re-accentuates in its own way the works of its most immediate past' (*The Dialogic Imagination* 420). This sentence anticipates the question, 'Why are the Victorians important to us?' and demonstrates that they can be oriented to the spirit of the age in which they find themselves recreated; in this case, the late twentieth century. The technical term used by Bakhtin for this is 'refraction'. A word is like a ray of light, which, in its trajectory, undergoes refraction because it passes through other voices and their connotations. The authorial discourse adjusts and determines the 'angle of refraction' of the word (*The Dialogic Imagination* 432).

Metafiction in Intertextuality: The Problem of Parody

Bakhtin's statement, 'Novelistic discourse is always criticizing itself' (*The Dialogic Imagination* 49), is a good introduction to the Victorianist novel. The issue of representation and the component of textual self-awareness comprise the primary markers between the Victorian and the Victorianist novels. Victorian novels rarely draw attention to the mode of representation; Jane Eyre can begin the last chapter of her narrative with the declaration, 'Reader, I married him' (*Jane Eyre*) without worrying that her mode of address may transport her reader out of the world of illusion to the real world, and remind him that he is only reading a book. There is no trace of irony in Jane's statement. The reader could be trusted not to let this mode of address startle him out of the life-likeness of the reading experience. However it is precisely this kind of a seam to which the reader of a Victorianist novel like *FLW* would remain alert.

Besides drawing attention to modes of representation, Victorianist novels, as already stated, also display their textual consciousness by juxtaposing genres so that the boundaries between them unmistakably mark them out as a) different and b) (just) texts. Thus, Byatt involves the dramatic monologue in *Possession* on the hypothesis that it is capable of transgressing Victorian boundaries and conveying deconstructive perspectives. The ballad is similarly situated in *Tess*. Tennant proffers her story as typical of the ballad genre in terms of theme, because both Hardy's novel as well as its Victorianist counterpart are ballad-like tales of betrayal, revenge and unrequited love. Either can be reduced to the simple bold outlines of a ballad in its essence.

FLW is a more elusive novel to categorise where generic representation is concerned. Its pressing aim is the larger issue of representing the Victorians, even though textual juxtaposition is not wholly absent from the novel. Fowles implies that a question like 'What is Victorian?' is out of place in the postmodernist clime. Instead one has to replace it with, 'What can be read as Victorian?'

This brings me to the question of the presence (or absence) of parody in Victorianism. The novel has a parodic tradition, from the European Cervantes to the British Fielding. Linda Hutcheon for her part maintains that Fowles parodies the Victorian convention of narrative omniscience by exposing the ludicrous bases of its assumptions in chapter thirteen of *FLW* (Hutcheon 57). Yet this is a lone example and is not, in any case, true of *Tess* or *Heathcliff*, which do not mock their source-texts, even while taking exception to them in several ways. Even Fowles does not parody the Victorian novel all the time. Moreover, even if the novel were parodying its Victorian self, this does not suggest an inadequacy of the genre. On the contrary, 'The novel form is almost boundless freedom. Throughout its history, the novel hasn't taken much advantage of that. It has missed out on that freedom' (Kundera 83). The Victorianist novels do take this advantage and display an amazing versatility.

It is in a similar vein that Fowles turns narrative omniscience, a typical convention of the Victorian novel, into a game in *FLW*. In his subversion of a traditional novelistic device, Fowles's retains the knowledge that this device was nevertheless appropriate for the period in which it was used. The celebrated chapter 13 shall bear repetition; having brought the story to the brink of a climactic revelation, the narrator disclaims knowledge and makes an uncharacteristic declaration, 'I do not know' (85). This is a classic 'metafictional case' of intertextuality; *Possession* on the other hand, displays 'generic cases' of intertextuality.

A closer look at the Victorianist novel's intertextual potential is directed through two novels, *Tess* and *FLW*.

Tess

When a reader approaches a conventional novel he acquiesces, at least for the duration of his reading, in the illusion that it projects a 'real' world. An important condition for novel reading is Coleridge's dictum of the 'willing suspension of disbelief'[4]. It is only when the reading process is completed that the reader acknowledges that the world which had entranced him into accepting as real, was actually, the imagination of the author.

In a metafictional text, however, the process works in reverse. The aim of metafiction is to disrupt the reader's involvement in the imaginary world conjured by the text, and make him conscious of his reading activity. One way of doing this is by mixing the categories of illusion and reality, so that fictional and real entities are made to impinge indiscriminately on each other. This transgression of traditionally respected boundaries between the real and the imaginary is a classic postmodern trait, and belongs to the category of its epistemological dominant (McHale 10). *Tess,* for example, experiments with various kinds of such infringement. In this novel, several beautiful women whose lives follow the same pattern of betrayal and murder, are grouped into what may be termed the 'Tess'–category. Some of these women are real, others imaginary. Yet Tennant alludes to all of them as though they could all inhabit the same world; by doing this she blurs a major distinction on which conventional understanding of literature rests. The alert reader finds that he has to continually re-align his perspective. At one instance he comes across a Tess from real life, like the actress who played the role of Tess Durbeyfield; and at another instance an imaginary character called Tess from Hardy's novel; both of whom are described as having been subject to chauvinistic treatment.

The various 'Tesses' in Tennant's novel may be catalogued as follows:

a) The literary stereotype, Tess, as established by Thomas Hardy in his novel. Tess Durbeyfield turned d'Urberville is seduced by Alec, deserted by Angel and dies on the gallows.
b) Augusta Way, the real-life model for Hardy's Tess. Her father, being Hardy's model for dairyman Crick, reinforces Augusta's kinship with Hardy's novel in *Tess of the d'Urbervilles*.
c) Augusta Way's daughter, also a real-life persona. Gertrude Bugler is a consummate actress who brings all Hardy's creations to life: Eustacia, Bathsheba; but none so perfectly and winningly as Tess.
d) The protagonist of Tennant's novel, also called Tess. Her story is narrated by Liza-Lu, whose name is identical with that of Tess Durbeyfield's sister in *Tess of the d'Urbervilles*.
e) Baby Tess – the 'you' of Tennant's novel, and a fictional character.

f) The Celtic warrior from legend/history, also called Tess.

'Tess' in Tennant's novel is therefore an intriguing entity with many ancestries. She is not just the sexual charmer of Hardy's creative imagination, but also an intellectual tease. Tess is a riddle who confuses the question of the real versus the imaginary. The metafictional drive of the novel is such that the real and the imaginary are shown as symbiotic, and the traditional answer that reality and illusion are mutually exclusive, does not hold. Tennant makes her point about the proselytising power of the imagination, by showing that fictions are extremely powerful, especially when they are confirmed by texts. Potent enough to permeate into life and infiltrate into the ranks of the real, fictions enable Tennant to declare of a real geographical place called 'Wessex', that 'the flippant seductions of Alec d'Urberville linger still in all this part of Dorset; and Tess's heart-rending voice, whether uttering the low diapason of the baptism of her dying child, or singing songs with the other dairymaids at Talbothays, still echoes when the winter wind whistles, when the larks sing on the high ground at Evershot' (Tennant 11).

One of the ways in which Tennant produces a novel union of reality and fiction is by the skilful re-adaptation of a character from *Tess of the d'Urbervilles*. In Hardy's novel, Liza-Lu, the sister of Tess, plays a marginal role in the story and briefly enters the main plot by marrying Angel Clare after her sister's death. Liza-Lu is also the name of the narrator of Tennant's novel; she too has a sister called Tess. This leads one to speculate whether Liza-Lu has a separate identity of her own at all, or whether she is merely a cross-textual acknowledgement of Hardy's prototype of 'the younger sister'.

This question comes to the fore in the dramatic enactment of *Tess of the d'Urbervilles*. In the play where Gertrude Bugler acts as Tess, Gertrude's sister plays the part of Liza-Lu, thereby joining two figures in one: the fictional character Liza-Lu, and the 'sister-figure'. The boundary-crossing between the realms of the real and the imaginary becomes active when Miss A. Bugler the *actress* ('Liza-Lu' of the play), falls in love with the *actor* who plays Angel Clare. In this she follows her textual destiny, though in a complicated manner; here is no straightforward love triangle, because the actor she loves is not Dr E. W. Smerdon, who plays the role of Angel in the same play. Rather, she has fallen in love with the *film star* who acts as Angel in a different production: 'Liza-Lu has chosen Conrad Nagel, Tess's co-star in the Goldwyn film, now showing at the picture palace in Dorchester' (Tennant 170). The boundaries that are transgressed are multiple, as more than one genre is involved. Characters from the novel(s), the play, and the movie, wander into each other's domains at will.

More follows. Liza-Lu alias A. Bugler, deeply in love with Nagel, begins to starve herself as a result of love-sickness. The plot of Hardy's novel is shown to have 'real-life' consequences, and becomes an example used by Tennant to underscore metafiction in her novel. It is usual for real-life happenings to dictate textual narratives, but Tennant appears to say that a movement in the reverse direction is no less plausible[5].

This idea becomes prominent in the context of the cock crowing, an event that has textual connotations dating from the Bible. The same incident is used by Tennant to make *Tess* both ballad-like and metafictional. Remarking on the crowing of the cock in the afternoon during one of the rehearsals, Tennant comments that 'great is the power of fantasy over reality' (162). Everyone in the team feels apprehensive and anticipates an unpleasant happening because in Hardy's novel, a cock crows, and later Angel and Tess learn that Retty Priddle has attempted suicide by drowning. Tennant takes this opportunity to endorse her novel's metafictional overtones: 'although *Tess* is *just a novel – and this is just* a rehearsal of an amateur dramatization of the novel – everyone there also feels as if they heard an omen of misfortune' (Tennant 160, emphasis mine)[6]. And as if on cue, Fred Beazer runs in to say that a girl has drowned herself off Chesil bank. For Tennant this incident also has an additional intertextual use of amplifying the ballad strains of *Tess*.

The intertextual implications of the above excerpt in Tennant's narrative are more than one:

a) Fiction can predate and, in a sense, even create reality, thereby inverting the normal procedure of life-generating text. This is one of the ways of generating metafiction, and Tennant uses it with great aplomb. Here is a metafictional move that, in fact, pushes fiction to the frontiers of metaphysics, as pointed out elsewhere in this book.
b) Although the reader is led to make the previous assumption on the basis of his belief in the 'reality' of Tennant's narrative, in fact Tennant's narrative is no more real than Hardy's. Tennant expects her reader to read *Tess* as though the events *it* narrates are 'real', but as though Hardy's is imaginary and fictional. However her metafictional manoeuvres eventually bring the reader to the realisation that this too is a novel, cohabiting the same space as *Tess of the d'Urbervilles*.
c) A textual collusion prevails between the novels of Hardy and Tennant, which prompts her to obliquely reinforce the power of the fictional. When she deploys the drowning incident as an echo from Hardy's narrative and makes it obey the same causal law as the original, she is reinforcing the power of texts in general, and Hardy's in particular.

A second site of intertextuality triggered by metafiction is found in the following sentence, 'There are pilgrims already to the famous sites, such as Wool Manor where Tess would have spent her wedding night if she had not confessed to Angel, or the cottage at Higher Bockhampton, where the poet suffered his humble childhood" (Tennant 133). Here again a mutual trespassing between fact and fiction transpires. In the same sentence a fictional incident describing Tess and her wedding night is treated on par with the historically real Hardy's childhood, as if to say that both require to be perceived and believed in the same way.

FLW

John Fowles's *FLW* is the most metafictional of the novels that we could place under the rubric of Victorian studies. By exposing the artifice of writing, metafiction foregrounds the divide between the 'real' and the 'fictional', and appears to repudiate the fundamental assumptions of mimesis. The most important of these assumptions is that the reader willingly (mis)takes the reading experience as a living experience, and allows himself to be affected by the events of the narrative as though they were events in the phenomenological world. Linda Hutcheon compromises with the possibility that metafiction is a violation of the mimetic code, by calling metafiction or self-reflexivity, a 'mimesis of process'. According to her, conventional realism is a 'mimesis of *product*' (Hutcheon 38), while metafiction or 'narcissistic fiction' is based on a 'mimesis of *process*' (Hutcheon 39). To her, 'Metafiction is still fiction. . . . Auto-representation is still representation' (Hutcheon 39).

The debate about realism and metafiction being antithetical modes of representation, however, persists. Intertextuality becomes significant in this debate since it disturbs accepted norms regarding representation. It focuses on textuality, drawing attention to the identity of the text as constructed with words, and not as a reflection of the world of real feelings and happenings. Intertextuality thereby complicates the mimetic postulate that a text is only an imitation of reality.

There is no doubt that metafiction shakes the foundations of the realistic tradition. Usually 'we speak of the novel as being "realistic" if it seems to reproduce the features of the world we live in, or at least the world man lives in or has lived in' (Johnson 289). Fowles introduces metafiction in an ingenious manner. His manner of doing this is by stretching realism to its utmost limit. When this happens, the effect of verisimilitude collapses, revealing realism as an artificial mode of representation and indicating that the novel is a text (and not reality). Johnson's thesis, in short, is that realism as a convention can succeed only if it stops short of being completely real. Total realism is self-defeating as it involves a display of its limits. One of Fowles's missions in *FLW* is to interrogate many of the naive assumptions underlying realism as an artistic creed.

Johnson points out that a realistic work attempts to reduce, as much as possible, 'the gap between the experience of art and the experience of life, to making the medium, the art work, so transparent that it disappears' (Johnson 289). But there is a paradox in this enterprise, which comes into operation when the gap is reduced to zero: instead of transparency, opaqueness ensues. 'In the realistic tradition,' says Johnson, 'the image must be made so that we think it looks like real life, but not so much so that we confuse it with real life' (294).

When Johnson refers to the emphasis of verisimilitude to 'an unseemly extent' (291), a word-play on 'seem' operates to suggest that realistic representation sets a clear limit on the extent of perception that the reader is allowed. The following examples from *FLW* show how metafiction arises from realism of this sort.

In chapter three of the novel, Fowles affixes the first of several footnotes. Charles, he says, was 'a healthy agnostic'. He then follows this sentence in the text with an asterisk, to explain in a note that Charles 'would not have termed himself so, for the very simple reason that the word was not coined (by Huxley) until 1870; by which time it had become much needed' (*FLW* 18). This move introduces anachronism, which is an anomaly studiously avoided by realistic novels depicting a bygone age. However, since the technique of *FLW* is postmodernist, Fowles not only violates chronology, but also draws attention to the violation. At this juncture let us cite Brian McHale's comments on postmodernist versions of history (McHale 84–96). According to him, the postmodernist novel would resort to precisely the sort of illusion-breaking techniques that the classical historical novel would avoid. One such technique is to contradict the official record of history with something so obviously preposterous, that the reader is shocked into the realisation that he is only [sic] reading a book. Another postmodernist technique is the deliberate flaunting of anachronism.

A word on Fowles's use of this footnote is also in order. The footnote is a text with an entirely different intent from that infused in it at this juncture by Fowles. Footnotes are used to buttress the text, but this particular one disrupts it. In any case, footnotes are rather misplaced in a work of fiction; in fiction, extraneous information from the world of reality would normally rupture the smoothness of representation. This is especially so when the information is placed on the same page as the narrative, as would be the case when the information is provided in a footnote. The juxtaposition of a note with the main body of the text is also an intertextual technique, as borders tend to get visually focused in such a proceeding.

Another much-quoted example from *FLW* of the limits of realism is chapter thirteen, where the narrator absolves himself of authorial omniscience, which is the characteristic Victorian mode of storytelling. He perversely withholds the innermost thoughts of his character Sarah from his reader on the ground that he 'does not know'. In addition, the narrator defends himself by confusing the division between illusion and reality: 'I have disgracefully broken the illusion? No. My characters still exist, and in a reality no less, or no more, real than the one I have just broken' (*FLW* 86–87).

On minor as well as major levels, the narrator periodically slips into his identity as real-life author, and intrudes upon the novel's world. This disconcerting procedure cautions the reader from losing himself in the amazingly Victorian-like world of *FLW*. Let us give an instance. In chapter thirty-six, after leaving the services of Mrs Poulteney, Sarah unwraps her purchases in a hotel room. One of them is a Toby jug. The narrator begins to depict it in realistic terms; but stretches it, gradually, to the point where it moves from the category of *realistic fiction* to that of *reality*, thereby disorienting the reader. Initially the Toby jug is described as 'not one of those garish-coloured monstrosities of Victorian manufacture, but a delicate little thing in pale mauve and primrose-yellow' (*FLW* 241). Thus far the representation is realistic. Then a detail is added: 'the Toby was cracked, and was to be re-cracked in the course of time, as *I* can testify, having bought it *myself* a year or two ago for a good deal more than the three pennies Sarah was charged' (*FLW* 241, emphases mine). This sentence breaks the illusion and produces metafiction since the narrator has already made it clear that his story is purely fictional, and has no autobiographical overtones that could tone his admission about the Toby jug as realistic.

So that, although on the face of it, this logic ought to make Sarah seem 'more' real, since she appears to share the world of the narrator, the reader quickly realises the absurdity of this notion. This is a clear case of realism that actually foregrounds the gap (while ostensibly trying to conceal it) between the world that the novel imitates, and its own textual status. In short, realism has failed by an act of over-reaching. Apart from objects like Sarah's jug, characters too are made to cross over from text to reality. In chapter eleven, Fowles plays a similar trick with Mary, Ernestina's maid. Her 'great-great-granddaughter, who is twenty-two years old this month I write in, much resembles her ancestor; and her face is known over the entire world, for she is one of the more celebrated younger English film actresses' (*FLW* 68–69).

Fowles harps persistently on the process of writing and representation so that his metafictional exercise has a high visibility status in the novel. F. N. Smith supplies an example with reference to Charles's valet: 'Sam could, did give the appearance, in some back taproom, of knowing all there was to know about city life' (quoted in Smith's 'Revision and the Style of Revision in *The French Lieutenant's Woman*' 89). Smith's study of the manuscripts of *FLW* shows that Fowles first wrote 'could' and then 'did'. Since the latter verb was a revision and replacement of the former, it is reasonable to enquire why he retained both tenses in the final version of the novel. One explanation in favour of the metafictional dynamics of *FLW* is that such a sentence mimics the very process of writing by conveying the image of a writer engaged in deep reflection, who is too engulfed by the demands of writing to pause for corrections. Bakhtin uses the image of scaffolding, which is subsequently removed, to describe the working of poetry (*The Dialogic Imagination* 331). A novel like *FLW*, on the other hand, retains the scaffolding: the foregoing instance is a case in point.

The most celebrated and discussed metafictional feature of *FLW* is its plural ending. Fowles in fact provides three conclusions. The first of these, which appears near the middle of the book, is generally discounted in arguments about metafiction. This is a conventional Victorian ending that appropriately removes Sarah, the 'other' woman, from the picture; and envisages a happy, if humdrum, life for Charles and Tina. But there is also a provision in the novel for dismissing this ending as Charles's daydreaming.

The final two endings appearing successively in chapters sixty and sixty-one have provoked much comment. Fowles is not entirely original in re-writing the ending of chapter sixty as chapter sixty-one. As Scruggs observes, 'In truth, Fowles may have consciously reversed the two endings of Dickens's novel, which he admits is one of his favourites' (Scruggs 96). The novel is *Great Expectations* (1860–61). In chapter fifty-nine of this novel, Pip and Estella are ostensibly joined together for life. Although no promises are made between them, and although their conversation is shot through with ambiguity, the concluding sentence of the novel is Pip's emphatic assertion, 'I saw no shadow of another parting from her' (*Great Expectations* 493).

Dickens however is understood to have originally planned an ending where Pip and Estella go their separate ways, but at the last minute changed his mind. This was purportedly on the request of his novelist–friend, Edward Bulwer-Lytton. Dickens was convinced by Bulwer-Lytton's reasons, as he told Forster later; 'I have put in as pretty a little piece of writing as I could, and I have no doubt the story will be more acceptable through the alteration' (quoted in *Great Expectations* 494).

Another Victorian novel with two endings is Hardy's *The Return of the Native* (1878) which 'offers in a footnote an unhappy ending to those with "an austere artistic conscience" ' (Conradi in '*The French Lieutenant's Woman*: novel, screenplay, film' 45).

For the Victorians, an 'acceptable' ending would be a conventional 'happy' one, particularly since they were troubled by agnosticism and social upheavals, and may well have craved for reassurance, even if only in the world of fiction. A century later, for the postmodernists, doubt is much more entrenched, and unhappiness more plausible than joy. The acceptable (because probable) ending for Fowles's readers would be the 'unhappy' one where Sarah and Charles part from each other.

Manuscripts of *FLW*, which Elizabeth Mansfield discusses with thoroughness in her article, reveal that originally the novel had only one ending: a happy one. It was at his wife's urging that Fowles incorporated a second ending in his novel. One way of regarding the double ending is as a defiant rejoinder and a postmodern replacement to the Victorian habit of novelistic closure (the examples I have provided of Dickens and Hardy are exceptions to the rule). At the same time, a double conclusion is also 'true to the Jekyll-and-Hyde Victorians as the author has depicted them throughout the book' (Smith, 'Revision and the Style of Revision in *The French Lieutenant's Woman*' 87). To ratify this interpretation, Smith quotes from *FLW*: 'Every Victorian had two minds' (quoted in Smith 87).

Moreover, unlike *Great Expectations* or *The Return of the Native*, the two endings of *FLW* compel the reader to acknowledge that an ending is an artifice, and that it can even be arbitrary. By virtue of their adjacent places, and also of their mutual exclusiveness, these endings leave no room for a realistic interpretation, and thereby officiate as excellent devices of metafiction. One ending has to be chosen at the expense of the other, for here is no straightforward case of an unhappy meeting between Sarah and Charles eventually ending happily.

The first ending of *FLW* in chapter sixty sees Charles and Sarah united. Chapter sixty-one seems to suggest a fresh beginning, intertextual in turn with the previous one. The plot reintroduces the bearded man, a persona of the narrator, who had earlier made an appearance in the novel (*FLW* 346–49). He has now come to turn the clock literally back. 'He makes a small adjustment to the time. It seems. . . that he was running a quarter of an hour fast. It is doubly strange, for there is no visible clock by which he could have discovered the error in his own timepiece' (*FLW* 395). Thence the reader is taken seven pages back in the narrative to the sentence in the previous chapter, 'No. It is as I say. You have not only planted the dagger in my breast, you have delighted in twisting it' (*FLW* 388, 395). This, Charles's accusation against Sarah, is revoked in this 'last' chapter to take a different, sadder route. By placing the weight of responsibility on the reader, who has to choose between the two 'last' chapters, Fowles is exercising his existentialist rights as well as forcing the reader to realise that metafiction is not just an intellectual game. For by being invited to take his pick of the endings, the reader is actually made to collaborate in the process of producing *FLW*.

Traditional Devices

What place do traditional means of assessing a genre such as plot, character and theme occupy in the Victorianist novels? The answer is that they reinstate these traditional devices, but with reservations. *FLW*, *Possession, Tess*, *WSS*, *Heathcliff*, and *Angels and Insects*, have clearly discernible plots. Since *Tess*, *WSS* and *Heathcliff* derive directly from single Victorian predecessors, this is perhaps inevitable. But this fact is true also of the other novels. Plot is perhaps indispensable in any simulation of the Victorian novel, since Victorian novels are firmly founded on plot. A social reformer like Charles Dickens could not eschew it, and even in her novels of psychological realism, George Eliot did not dispense with it. Not even an experimental novel like *Wuthering Heights* could discard it; in fact, much of Emily Bronte's experimentation is in the realm of plot. Hardy, of course, depended greatly on his plots to enforce his vision of tragic destiny.

The Victorianist novel retains this legacy, but juggles with it by anachronising, metafictionalising and textualising it; in short, loading the Victorian novel with postmodern modes of perception and representation. Thus, even while making a token acknowledgement of the Aristotelian yardsticks of plot and character, the Victorianist novel goes well ahead of these counters. Since the Victorianist novel is also fundamentally deconstructionist, plot and character become secondary issues, giving way to the larger interests of irony, textuality and the nature of academic writing. In the final analysis, the Victorianist novelists exhibit insights that defamiliarise. The effect aimed at and frequently achieved by the Victorianist novel is the unsettling experience of *déja-vu*.

NOTES

1 'The death of the novel has been much discussed for a long time: notably by the Futurists, by Surrealists, by nearly all the avant-gardes'. Milan Kundera, *The Art of the Novel*, trans. Linda Asher (London: Faber and Faber Ltd., 1988) 13.

2 In his book, *The Dialogic Imagination* (p. 263), Mikhail Bakhtin gives the term 'heteroglossia' to the multiplicity of social voices which enter the novel through the interplay between authorial speech, the speech of the narrator, inserted genres and the speech of the character.

3 'The novel permits the incorporation of various genres, both artistic (inserted short stories, lyrical songs, poems, dramatic scenes etc.) and extra-artistic (everyday rhetorical, scholarly, religious genres and others)'. Bakhtin in fact goes as far as to say, 'it is difficult to find any genres that have not at some point been incorporated into a novel by someone'. *The Dialogic Imagination,* ed. Michael Holquist, trans. Caryl Emerson and Michael Holquist (Austin: University of Texas Press, 1981) 302–21.

4 Coleridge describes his creative endeavours in the *Lyrical Ballads* as an attempt to 'procure for these shadows of imagination that willing suspension of disbelief for the moment, which constitutes poetic faith' in chapter 14 of *Biographia Literaria*. D. J. Enright and Ernst de Chickera, eds. *English Critical Texts* (Delhi: Oxford University Press, 1975) 191.

5 This inference rests on the assumption that the events in Tennant's novel are 'real' – which they are only in the mimetic frame of perception. If the reader begins to see the characters of Tennant's novel as fictional figures, then the notion of text directing life becomes invalid. Tennant's success depends on the reader's ability to stop just short of acknowledging that 'all is fiction'. He must see Hardy's novel as a text, but not Tennant's novel.

6 The *Tess* she refers to here is Hardy's novel, not her own.

4 Gender and Intertextuality

There exists a homonymous relationship between the two terms 'genre' and 'gender', which reinforces the consummate intertextual roles that both fulfil in Victorianist novels. *Harrap's Compact Dictionnaire* enumerates five English meanings for the French word 'genre'. One of these, the grammatical, is 'gender' (177)[1]. The intertextual agenda for Victorianist fiction remains incomplete without a discussion of gender. All the novels of this study reveal a predilection for considering this issue, whether tangentially or assertively.

While accounting for gender in texts, it may be necessary to take into consideration the sex as well as the gender-politics of the respective author in the argument. Tennant's *Tess* suggests this by asserting that Hardy's feminist politics is suspect because he is a man after all. However much he may have showed himself feminist in the creation of Tess Durbeyfield, he was anything but kind to the women in his life. However, the corollary of this inference, that a woman writer is always sympathetic to the condition of the woman, need not follow, as Jean Rhys shows in *WSS*. This novel makes the interesting revelation that a woman, even a feminist, writer does not necessarily write a feminist novel.

Studies of gender invariably lead one to the rich area of gender-politics. According to Elaine Showalter, gender and its politics are inextricably intertwined with language. The English language affords a good illustration of her point, where despite the presence of a neuter gender, the masculine form remains the universal norm. 'We can call either Sylvia Plath or Robert Lowell a "poet", but we can not call Lowell a "poetess" except as an insult' (*Speaking of Gender* 1).

The issue of gender in textuality accrues semantic layers owing to indeterminacy regarding related terms like 'sex', 'feminism' and 'gender'. Unlike sex, which is biologically determined, gender is a construct. Interestingly enough, gender-identity is based upon the notion of differentiality and thereby similar to Saussurean descriptions of language.

Feminist studies are extensive, and feminist opinions range from the radical to the moderate; within feminism there are at least two, mutually irreconcilable views, which are raised here as they are important for this chapter. One view maintains that gender-awareness is a consequence of feminism, and that gender studies are concerned with man–woman relations. On the other hand, feminist studies centre themselves exclusively on the woman. A fall-out of this is that feminist readings of a text would be less objective than gender-oriented ones.

The other point of view is that feminism and gender studies are not mutually restrictive. The two terms 'gender' and 'feminism' shall be deployed synonymously in the course of this chapter except when otherwise demanded by a singular context. Gender is the larger criterion within which the feminist impulse is studied: such is the line of this reasoning.

Gender and the Victorians

Gender is a keynote of Victorianism, and in his essay on trends in Victorian studies George Levine is prompted to observe, 'Perhaps the most important critical development out of Victorianism was feminism' (Levine 140). The 'woman question' was of enormous significance to the Victorians. 'From the 1830s onwards Victorian Britain was obsessively concerned with the Woman Question as they called it. . . No single cultural myth prevailed and the idea of 'Woman', her 'mission', her 'sphere' and her 'influence' became a site of struggle where competing ideologies strove for dominance' (Thomas 238). Not the least because women had also started articulating for the first time in significantly large numbers, during the era of Queen Victoria.

In Victorian England controversies raged over women's education, suffrage and economic condition. The age saw a distinguished line of women writers. Other fields besides literature also reflected female talent. These were as diverse as prison reform (Elizabeth Fry being an outstanding representative), sociology (Beatrice Webb), mathematics and computing (Ada Lovelace), medicine (Elizabeth Anderson); and in nursing, traditionally allotted to women, Florence Nightingale worked a revolution.

The question of how women were represented in texts produced in such a clime becomes imbued with significance. It is natural to expect a degree of difference between the representations of women by male writers and those by females, and anticipate prejudice, perhaps even unfair portrayal, in the case of the former[2]. Yet, individual texts disclose that the textual character of gender is not so simplistic or reductionist as suggested by the above conjecture. While Dickens's angelic heroines may well subscribe to Victorian male fantasies of female submissiveness, where does a militantly feminist novel like *Tess of the d'Urbervilles*, also engendered by a male writer, accommodate itself?

A plethora of such quiescent subtexts invade readings of gender in textuality, which are brought to light in Victorianist re-writings of Victorian narratives. A brief consideration of two examples is warranted at this juncture, both of which shall find elaborate and individual analyses later on: Emma Tennant's *Tess* and Jean Rhys's *WSS*. In *Tess*, Tennant denounces Hardy as a perpetrator of crimes against women, by insidiously adopting the guise of their protector. The most basic information required to process the implications of a gender-based reading here is as follows: Tennant is a woman plus Victorian*ist*; whereas Hardy is male, and Victorian. While this fact by itself would equip Tennant with an advantageous position to foster the feminist cause of gender, a difficulty poses itself in the form of Hardy's much-touted feminist leanings. Tennant overcomes it by converting Hardy's feminist championship from an assertion into a query, whose answer she supplies with a categorical negative.

One has also to remember another factor in discussions of intertextuality and gender, which is invaluable in an appraisal of Victorianist perspectives. This is the great chasm between the status of woman in the nineteenth and the late (or even mid) twentieth centuries. What may have been radically feminist for the Victorians may in all likelihood constitute the norm in the present era. Fowles makes precisely this point in his portrayal of Sarah in *FLW*. She is a Victorian anomaly simply because she is ahead of her times; to borrow a metaphor from Darwin, she embodies female evolution. The reason Sarah was a misfit in the Victorian era was that she had already evolved into the twentieth century.

But in her indictment of Hardy as brazenly patriarchal, Tennant appeals not to standards that are historically contingent but universal and timeless, and she employs the generic grid of the ballad to represent the continuing nature of female persecution by men.

Although Rhys too would write as both Victorianist and woman, her task is more formidable since the Victorian text that she challenges, was also authored by a woman. Therefore, like Tennant, Rhys too has the Herculean task of repudiating the feminist leanings of her Victorian author in the process of establishing the authenticity of her perception. *WSS* is an early example of what Showalter means by proposing that 'talking about gender without a commitment to dismantling sexism, racism, and homophobia can degenerate into nothing more than a talk show' (*Speaking of Gender* 10). Jean Rhys faithfully highlights the social politics that insidiously operate inside the plot of *Jane Eyre*, which can uphold a Jane while humiliating a Bertha. The knowledge that a woman authored *Jane Eyre*, can only subject it to more rigorous scrutiny under the rule of gender.

Gender is latent in constructions of masculinity no less than femininity. Is Rochester truly 'macho'? Or is he a self-seeking coward? This is one of the questions that *WSS* puts to the readers of *Jane Eyre*. For her part Tennant does not even raise the topic of Angel Clare's callousness or culpability. Without any dispute, the narrative of *Tess* claims these for him, going to the length of summarily disposing of his twentieth-century counterpart in a few pages.

In the following pages we shall look at the way in which the question of gender is wrought into the fabric of a few Victorianist texts.

Possession

Possession ingeniously displays the enabling role of gender in the Victorianist novel. The orchestrations between gender and intertextuality produce various texts within *Possession*; notable among which are feminist (creative) writing and feminist criticism. Though its Victorian setting qualifies it to be a historical novel, a metafictional dimension as well as generic proliferation help the novel to reach a plane of sophistication that is denied to the traditional historical novel. Feminist critical theory which informs *Possession*, also poses the same danger for the multifacetedness of *Possession*, that the genre of the historical novel can. Feminism is impelled by a cause, which endows its text with a monotonic cast. If *Possession* retains its interactive character despite the deployment of a fairly forceful feminist text within its covers, it is because of a self-questioning, and not necessarily a self-validating note that it assigns to gender.

Various sites of gender-study present themselves for identification in this novel. Christabel LaMotte's poems, Ellen Ash's journal and Sabine de Kercoz's diary are but a few cases of gender-consciousness in *Possession*. LaMotte's epic *Melusina* is a sustained poetic narrative that meticulously follows the lines of conventional feminism in its theme and style, and effortlessly offers itself as an instance of conventional feminist perception. Having initially provided a substantial corpus of text (in the above-mentioned examples) that can be unmistakably recognised as feminist, Byatt thereafter proceeds to undercut some of the principal assumptions of orthodox feminism. Her major devices for this are the comical feminist character Leonora Stern, and the ambivalent dramatic monologue, 'Mummy Possest', which foregrounds a powerful feminist signifier in the séance.

A search for the regular, straightforward feminist texts in *Possession* reveals the most forceful of all feminists in the novel to be Christabel LaMotte, who partakes of the poetic character of two real-life nineteenth-century poetesses. This is expounded at length in the chapter,

'Intertextual Devices'. One is Christina Rossetti, whose name partially resonates with Christabel's; the other is Emily Dickinson, whose staccato style is clearly evinced in Christabel's poems, and whose feminist strain is vehement in such lines as,

> My subject is Spilt Milk.
> A white Disfigurement
> A quiet creeping Sleek
> Of squandered Nourishment (*Possession* 381)

Ellen Ash is also a latent feminist in whose writing simmers a classic feminist rage, born as a consequence of male suppression. The culprit is not, as one might expect, her husband Ash, but the ubiquitously male-dominated period which barely tolerated female talent. In her personal life Ellen conforms to patriarchal rules, but her journal, a 'lesser genre' (Gilbert and Gubar 72), contains tell-tale signs of stifled poetic ambition. 'I wanted to be a Poet and a Poem, and now am neither, but the mistress of a very small household' (*Possession* 122). While there is no overt trace of an accusation against her husband anywhere in Ellen's diary, the reader has to keep in mind that she would be cautious to preserve appearances even in a journal.

Ellen's desire to be a poem (as well as a poet) is a pointer towards feminist arguments concerning male imposition. Gilbert and Gubar aver that patriarchal texts have perforce been compulsory looking glasses for women to 'see' themselves in (Gilbert and Gubar 17). The looking glass as a familiar image to describe the office of literature is as old as Plato (Plato 346). Conceptually, the mirror conveys a latent principle of feminism that male texts 'show' women (albeit in a distorted fashion) but stifle their voices. A consequence of such showing is that often women, who are supposed to see themselves in these looking glasses, fail to recognise their own selves as a result of the distortion they undergo in male ways of seeing. Thus in the hands of a male writer, the text also becomes a successful silencer of the woman's voice.

Possession furthermore shows that circumstances have not altered even a century after Ellen. The career of Beatrice Nest, who is one of the twentieth-century characters in the novel, is delineated as proof of this assumption. As a doctoral candidate Beatrice was discouraged from writing a dissertation on Ash's masterpiece, *Ask to Embla*. Instead, her energies were forcibly diverted towards editing Ellen Ash's journal. This decision taken on her behalf by the higher academic powers-that-be (needless to add, male) is based not so much on the presumption that a woman would be able to do greater justice to a woman writer's diary, as on the characteristically male perspective that being a woman researcher, Beatrice would do less than justice to a male poet.

This narrative inset obeys another principle of feminism in that a female bonding is forged between Beatrice and Ellen. The journal is a 'female' textual domain, and only another female can decipher it. Gradually, through her reading of Ellen's diary, Beatrice becomes implicated in Ellen's life, and empathises with her by participating in the injustice of her situation. This empowers her to read between Ellen's dutiful-sounding sentences. 'She became aware of the mystery of privacy, which Ellen, for all her expansive ordinary eloquence, was protecting, it could be said' (*Possession* 115).

Since the novel takes pains to convey that Beatrice is not a professed feminist, additional authenticity is imparted to her interpretation of Ellen's journal. In this manifestation gender delineates an unusual textual feature: that within the journal, writing is not only a means of expression, but also of suppression and hiding.

There are at least two Victorian texts in *Possession* that become intertextual on account of their incorporation of a gender-based perspective. These are examples of undeflected intertextuality, whose proselytising feminism is beyond doubt. They are LaMotte's narratives, 'The Glass Coffin' and *Melusina,* which we shall examine in some detail.

Nested as it is within the novelistic narrative of *Possession*, 'The Glass Coffin' already holds an intertextual status. It is a chameleon-text, which is a fairy tale as well as a feminist parable. At first sight its narrative line declares an allegiance with the story of Snow White and the Seven Dwarves as anatomised by Gilbert and Gubar (36–43). LaMotte's version is a feminist re-writing of this overtly patriarchal fairy tale[3].

After a long search, the tailor-hero of 'The Glass Coffin' reaches the place where the heroine is imprisoned. In the beautiful girl sleeping inside the coffin, the tales of Snow White and Sleeping Beauty converge. It may be recalled that Snow White's wicked stepmother also puts her inside a glass coffin, mistakenly assuming her to be dead.

The heroine is obviously lying there waiting for a sexual awakening; but the tailor only chastely kisses her on the cheek. This point sharply marks the way this story turns against its predecessor-text of Snow White, whose narrative is structured by male desire and the will to control. First of all, the 'hero' here is no prince, but a mere tailor; and the lady he rescues is much superior to him in station. A second line of feminist protest is located in the creation of the wicked male magician who has incarcerated her. He is a figment of the female imagination and a replacement to Snow White's stepmother. If preserving the 'angel' in the house was a prevailing Victorian male fantasy, the magician who all but kills this heroine is a female judgement on the cruelty of male fantasy. The concluding section of this tale enlarges upon a distinctly female fantasy when after being rescued and restored to liberty, the heroine continues to live exactly as she did before her marriage. In a pointed reversal of narrative expectation, after offering to marry her the tailor tells the beautiful girl, ' "I trust you will feel free to reconsider the matter, and remain, if you will, alone and unwed" ' (*Possession* 66). So she goes hunting with her brother while the tailor stays at home plying his craft. Here is another role-reversal, with the hero staying indoors and the heroine free to roam where her fancy chooses.

The introduction of a brother into the narrative seems counter-feminist, but the role he plays is glaringly innocuous. He has no power over his sister – not even to save her from the magician. He is also a twin brother; hence she is not bound by the law of primogeniture to obey him. In her role as 'sister', she is the co-ruler of their realm, which is neither 'the realm of domesticity' nor 'a miniaturized kingdom' like Snow White's (Gilbert and Gubar 40), but an extensive one.

In invoking the spectre of sexuality, Byatt partly resorts to a patently Victorian stereotype, and partly creates a specific kind of intertextuality that depends on gender to make its meaning complete. This intertextuality is manifested in a circumlocute fashion, where Christabel becomes a fictional correspondent to Christina Rossetti. In *Possession*, Maud, the twentieth-century heroine, remarks to her associate Roland that LaMotte's tales 'derived from Grimm and Tieck, with an emphasis on animals and insubordination' (*Possession* 52). About 1823, the first translation of *Grimms' Fairy Tales* took the Victorian reading public by storm; and Christina Rossetti's 'Goblin Market' (1862) which is a curious amalgam of fantasy and gender, is surely another parent text for Christabel's 'The Glass Coffin' and *Melusina*. Fairy tales 'partake of their historical contexts and reflect the dominant economic and political structures at the time of their origin, their retelling, their recording, or their creation' (Campbell 396). Campbell places 'Goblin Market' in sharp focus 'as an exploration of the limits defined by the Victorians for sexual roles, an investigation of gender identity' (Campbell 402). The narrative of 'The Glass Coffin' challenges these limits.

Both 'The Glass Coffin' and *Melusina* use gender as an intertextual principle to link Christabel with Christina. In a carefully crafted narrative like *Possession*, intertextuality requires to be founded on matters more profound than mere nomenclatural similarity. This is where thematic resonance becomes important. Sexual self-sufficiency on the part of the woman is a major theme of 'Goblin Market'. In *Possession* LaMotte's epic and fairy tales reinforce the independence of woman, while her personal life reflects this independence as well as a possible lesbian affair with Blanche.

LaMotte's epic *Melusina* is a product of the female desire for complete sexual autonomy. Such autonomy is achieved in lesbianism, which is complete and fulfilling in itself. *Melusina* is first described for the reader in Ellen Ash's words as 'a huge, intricately embroidered tapestry in a shadowed stone hall' (*Possession* 121). We may pertinently recall *Tess* at this juncture, where the act of narration is equated with weaving tapestry. Melusina who is a fish/serpent below the waist, is described as a monster by men. However, according to the female aesthetic, she is defined as beautiful, with a form that fascinates rather than repels. Ellen speaks for all women when she remarks of Melusina, 'Perhaps the most surprising touch is that the snake or fish is beautiful' (*Possession* 121).

The heroines who feature in the epic *Melusina* are all women who have suffered from male tyranny such as Medusa, Scylla, Hydra, and the Sphinx[4]. Why has their lot been tragic suffering? The answer is unequivocal in its indictment of patriarchy: 'But let the Power take a female form/And 'tis the Power is punished' (*Possession* 292). The wish to punish the female in authority is a consequence of the male fear of female power and female sexuality. Victorian women writers perceived this with clarity; in *Possession* not only Christabel, but also her French cousin, Sabine de Kercoz, registers this fact (*Possession* 354).

Raimondin's journey, like that of the tailor in 'The Glass Coffin', is rewarded with a female figure at his destination, the beautiful lady Melusina herself who is found singing. Melusina's song allegorically signifies art and creativity, and in entrusting her with the power of song, Christabel reinforces the feminist turn of her text by implying that imaginative acts are the female's prerogative.

Christabel's employment of the image of gazing, particularly in *Melusina*, is important also for Byatt to lay her foundation of gender-politics. Intertextuality presupposes a prior view at a text, which is re-assessed on the basis of this earlier glimpse. Byatt achieves a symbiotic association between gender and intertextuality, when she informs the act of looking with a symbolic significance. For centuries, literary tradition has granted to the male the right to regard and represent the world. But, according to the feminists, he has misappropriated trust by causing the balance to tilt against woman in textual representations. A gender-informed reading of *Melusina* reveals an implicit parallel between male-oriented writing and Raimondin's unlawful act of gazing at his wife, despite being expressly forbidden from doing so. In the words of Maud Bailey, who is the feminist critic in the twentieth-century world of *Possession* and also an authority on the poetry of Christabel LaMotte, when Melusina married Raimondin she 'made a pact that he would never spy on her on Saturdays' (*Possession* 33). Raimondin breaks this pact out of curiosity. The illegitimacy of Raimondin's act is emphasised by the use of the word 'spying'. With this incident LaMotte engineers a new Fall myth, where culpability is placed squarely on the shoulders of the man: *he* transgresses the command, *he* breaks his word.

It is a point of overwhelming significance for the feminist politics of *Possession* that until Raimondin perceives Melusina as a witch she remains undefined except as a beautiful woman. This feature functions as a paradigm for understanding the nature of textuality itself, whose identity rests on self-awareness. Feminists of *Possession*'s twentieth-century plot see Melusina as magnificently androgynous, certainly not as an anomaly. It takes a man, with his essentially male way of perception, to castigate her for her anatomical peculiarity. The gaze thereby becomes a means of bifurcating literary representation. As a watershed it paves the way for a development of two distinct and mutually hostile literary traditions based on gender. Christabel articulates to Sabine the question that Melusina raises: 'Who knows what Melusina was in her freedom with no eyes on her?' (*Possession* 373).

The Séance

Rightly apprehending the séance as a signifying web of Victorian cultural trends, feminist preoccupations and scientific controversies, Byatt foregrounds it to foster the politics of gender in *Possession* as well as *Angels and Insects* (in 'The Conjugial Angel'). In itself the séance is a performance of short duration, but its implications and cultural inheritances are tremendous. It was greatly in vogue during the Victorian period. Mrs Papagay, a character in the latter novella, innocently vocalises an essentially Victorianist inquiry when she asks, 'Why had the Dead just now, just recently, with such persistence, chosen to try to break back into the land of the living with raps, taps, messages, emanations, materialisations, spirit-flowers and travelling book-shelves?' (*Angels and Insects* 170).

Spiritualism, as the issue came to be known in the Victorian period, was a problematic notion. The word itself is uneasily close to 'spirituality'. But their semantics are diametrically opposed, the one suggesting the occult, and the other, theology. The ambivalence intrinsic to spiritualism is reinforced when one recalls that for these very powers, women were burnt at the stake in the sixteenth and seventeenth centuries.

In the Victorian period spiritualism earned the respect of such intellectuals as Lady Byron, Ada Lovelace, Elizabeth Barrett Browning, and Emily Jesse. In other words, it boasted a female following. Historically, the Victorian women's movement and women's involvement with the séance were separated by a span of only four months (Basham 122). 'Amidst the controversy that still surrounds the Victorian séance, one item of discussion remains incontrovertible:

– and that is, that the body of evidence which exists in relation to its claims is a female body' (Basham 121).

The gender-politics of the séance suggests that in an age that discredited religion and spirituality, women not very surprisingly staked a claim for authority in spheres similar to these in the domain of non-rationality. When the male-dominated bastion of mysticism and supernatural knowledge was toppled unwittingly by the Industrial Revolution and the discoveries of Darwin, men naturally shifted to the new site of power, which was science. For Victorian women to occupy the discarded site was also a natural move.

The séance, through which women ostensibly communicated with the dead, bestowed upon them a channel for self-expression and a means of fulfilment. It also empowered them. The medium of a séance laid claim to exclusive knowledge, which was a source of power. This claim did not always go uncontested. Disrupters of the séance, who 'grabbed' spirit-manifestations with the altruistic intention of unearthing malpractice were usually men. Browning, and Ash in *Possession*, violently interrupt séance proceedings from a conviction of their fraudulence. Despite such interruptions women persisted in conducting and attending séance-sittings. The séance thus held sway over a distinctly female space. Its advantage was that it could be practised from within the precincts of the home; indeed, only from within. The speaker-medium in 'Mummy Possest' says precisely:

> Know you not that we Women have no Power
> In the cold world of objects Reason rules,
> Where all is measured and mechanical? (*Possession* 410)

The séance as a metaphor also symbolises the suppressed female desire to write and her supposed powers of intuition. In the Victorian age the séance was held to have promoted automatic writing. In 'The Conjugial Angel', Mrs Papagay and Sophy Sheekhy are the conduits for the ghost of Arthur Hallam to give vent to his feelings and express his indignation over Emily Tennyson's marriage, which he considers as an instance of disloyalty on her part to his memory. Under the influence of his spirit, these mediums write as if possessed, with no volition of their own but guided entirely from outside. The séance as a feminist site of power is explored intensively by Byatt in the dramatic monologue in *Possession*, 'Mummy Possest'.

'Mummy Possest'

By abjuring a straightforward feminist argument even while drawing upon the substantial body of feminist thought, 'Mummy Possest' introduces a novel kind of intertextuality that partakes of self- questioning. From the perspective of reading for gender, the question that 'Mummy Possest' provokes is: what has Byatt achieved by making the medium female? The answer is likely to surprise: Byatt has debunked the feminist privileging of the female, in her representation of the medium in 'Mummy Possest', the dramatic monologue supposedly written by Ash.

The essentially feminist belief that a woman is endowed with supra-rational faculties which the male does not possess, is turned on its head in this poem. One way in which this happens is through the intertextual context of 'Mummy Possest'. This dramatic monologue derives from a prior text, Browning's dramatic monologue, 'Mr Sludge, "the Medium" '. The medium in Browning's poem is a male whose ostensible powers of communicating with the dead are discredited, and Sludge's monologue is a result of his being discovered in the act of deception. Byatt's transformation of a male medium to female could have been turned to great feminist advantage. Instead it seems calculated to discountenance the feminist agenda. Byatt endangers the feminist cause because in her poem the female speaker is no less duplicitous in her profession than Sludge.

It is also important to reflect on the fact that Byatt authors 'Mummy Possest' through Randolph Ash. In his 'real' life, Ash has been shown to have an aversion towards mediums, and a native distrust of their genuineness. It naturally follows that he would promote an unflattering representation of a medium in his poem. Nevertheless, Byatt could have overcome this obstacle by having Ash introduce a male medium on the lines of Sludge. Her transformation of a male medium to a female has inevitable interpretative repercussions.

The spuriousness of the medium in 'Mummy Possest' is incontrovertibly confirmed. In fact the speaker in 'Mummy Possest' takes unfair advantage of the fact that women are generally believed to be tuned into the world of spirits more easily than men are. This enables her to recognise the séance as a locus of power as well as an opportunity for women to demand a status on par with men:

> Here we have Power, here the Irrational,
> Where left is right, and clocks go widdershins,
> And women sit enthroned and wear the robes, . . . (*Possession* 410)

Through the speaker of this monologue, Ash (like Browning) suggests that the medium's knowledge is nothing but judiciously gathered items of gossip. Carefully docketed in memory to produce at the right moment, this was, for practical purposes, classified information and knowledge that granted power. The medium in

'Mummy Possest' is unscrupulous about misusing her knowledge and giving it the façade of spiritualist communing.

Byatt refuses to make a categorical comment on the issue, because she also concedes that there can be genuine mediums, such as Sophy Sheekhy in 'The Conjugial Angel', which the speaker of 'Mummy Possest' obliquely acknowledges. 'The force is fitful, and the vital spark / Which kindles in the Medium. . .' is 'flickering' (*Possession* 406).

In 'Mummy Possest', Byatt's undertaking is coloured by an ambivalence which is missing in the more strident statement on feminism that she makes through Leonora Stern. It is true that the author of 'Mummy Possest', Ash, is prejudiced against mediums. Hence his representation of one has to be accepted with reservations. This is especially the case since his poem is said to have been inspired by a real-life experience in which he publicly attacked Hella Lees, whose capabilities as a medium are neither disputed nor confirmed by the omniscient narrator. Meanwhile his attack on Mrs Lees is accessible to the reader only through her autobiography, which text may well give a biased account. And since the omniscient narrator is missing from this scene, it becomes difficult to tell whether Ash is prejudiced or Lees is misrepresenting the case. But at least this incident explains why Ash represented a spurious medium in his dramatic monologue. The question that remains is about Byatt's own position.

If Byatt had committed herself in this instance, a more definite statement in terms of gender could have been deduced from this dramatic monologue. But in characteristically postmodern and intertextual terms, Byatt uses more than one text (the autobiography, the narrative world of *Possession* and 'Mummy Possest') to consider the question of sincerity in a medium, and invests it with layers of ambiguity[5].

In the final analysis it is Byatt who holds the strings of *Possession.* The case may be argued for feminism by the observation that Hella Lees is not openly discredited, in which case 'Mummy Possest' becomes Ash's prejudiced outpouring. But it is possible to pursue this line of questioning further and ask why Byatt did not create a Mr Lees, a male medium like Sludge.

The Politics of Feminism: Leonora Stern in *Possession*

The introduction of Leonora Stern, American feminist critic, into the narrative of *Possession* brings Byatt closest to the creation of a reactionary text in terms of gender. By making Stern vulnerable to ridicule, both in the inconsistency of her ideological beliefs and in her unstable personality, Byatt parodies the quintessence of feminism. In the life and career of Leonora Stern, Byatt combines questions of gender and intertextuality, and goes a long way towards proffering one possible answer to the question, 'How is intertextuality advanced through gender?'

Here it is advanced through parody. Byatt's methods of parody deviate slightly from the norm but it is undeniably through a parodying of feminism that intertextuality is accredited. In general, parody initiates the following process. First, the text to be parodied is introduced, by methods such as imitation or partial quotation. Thereafter the reader's expectations are frustrated by producing a deviant and incongruous version from the original text (Rose 171).

In *Possession* Professor Stern of Tallahassee is presented as the only twentieth-century authority on LaMotte besides Maud Bailey. Her profile is caricatured for the reader even before she makes a personal appearance. George Bailey, who proves to be the unexpected means of Maud and Roland's access to the Ash–Christabel correspondence, alludes to Leonora in severely disparaging terms: 'There was a frightful nosy American. . . . Covered with paint and jangling jewellery, a real mess, she was. Wouldn't go when I asked her politely. Had to wave the gun at her' (*Possession* 79).

Already the reader's sympathy for any cause that Leonora may espouse is forfeited; instead the reader is guided to regard her as comic. Comedy is intrinsic to parody. Since Byatt makes Leonora a target for laughter, the integrity of feminism is compromised, for in Leonora's exaggerated loyalties and extreme positions the prototypical feminist comes to be parodied.

Leonora's letter to Maud (*Possession* 139–40), informing her of the Australian meeting of the Sapphic society, is a pattern of feminist vocabulary interspersed with such phrases as, 'the study of the female erotic in nineteenth-century poetry and the strategies and subterfuges through which it had to present or discover itself', and a crowning shibboleth, the suspected 'lesbian sexuality' of LaMotte (*Possession* 139).

Spectacular in appearance, Leonora's personal life is no less colourful. She turns her back on a happy marriage with Nathaniel Stern and enlists with the feminists. Nathaniel himself tries in vain to placate the feminists in his writings. Byatt capitalises on the intertextual scope of *Possession* to mock Nathaniel's efforts in her omniscient voice. 'Twenty years later he was still working on it, disapproved of by everyone, particularly the feminists' (*Possession* 311). The joke here is on both Nathaniel's fruitless attempts to appease feminism as well as the obduracy of the feminists. Surely there is something immature about cherishing such ideological enmity, and by stressing the childishness of the feminists rather than their commitment, the narrative voice introduces an aside, which highlights the intertextual process.

This parodic undertone gathers momentum in the delineation of Leonora's subsequent career. Having discarded an amenable, tractable husband like Nathaniel, who comes closest to the feminist dream of a cooperative husband, she lives with Saul Drucker who regularly beats her. The reader understands that Leonora lives with Drucker not despite his anti-feminist, cave-man tactics, but because of these. Leonora's tempestuous lifestyle with Drucker is nothing short of a disavowal of feminist principles. While promoting the right of women to be autonomous, if not authoritative, Leonora simultaneously encourages male aggression towards herself. Since this is tantamount to hypocrisy, feminism is thereby turned into an object of scorn.

The feminist text is a corpus that is cross-textual, as feminists borrow each other's terms, ideas and beliefs. This interchange enables a foundation-text of feminist language to exist as an identifiable text that can be recognisably parodied. We have previously drawn attention to the jargon. Another example from *Possession* is Stern's book, *Motif and Matrix in the Poems of LaMotte*, from which Roland reads excerpts.

The irony underlying Byatt's account of Stern's endeavours is finally clinched by the denouement of *Possession*, where Maud Bailey (and not Leonora) is acclaimed for having made fruitful discoveries and correct interpretations. The novel singles Maud out as the rightful literary heir as well as a literal descendant of Christabel LaMotte and Ash. Although Maud too is a feminist, her moderate approach does not elicit the mocking tone that Leonora's rabid missionary zeal excites.

Tess

Tess is a militant novel that challenges the feminist assumptions of its predecessor-text *Tess of the d'Urbervilles*, and its author, Thomas Hardy. The mainspring of Tennant's thesis is the startling divide between Hardy's fictions and his personal life. On the one hand, a tremendous conviction seems to be implied in his indignant record of the patriarchal exploitation of a Tess. On the other hand, the same Hardy brought misery and heartache to his first and second wives through the passion that he cherished for the several women who successively played the character of Tess in his life.

As the reader registers this new Hardy, he is provoked to wonder whether Tennant's intertextual method transgresses literary convention, for she seems to use 'life' as the yardstick of measuring (a) text. However, Tennant successfully overcomes any objection in this regard in two ways. First, she eschews a simplistic equation between life and text.

Instead, she uses metafiction as an ingenious means of bringing life and text into play with each other. We have illustrated this with examples in the chapter, 'The Novel'. Tennant's task is to bring two traditionally unrelated schemes of reference together in *Tess*. One consists of the fictional character Tess Durbeyfield; created by Thomas Hardy, she is a 'textual' (as different from a 'real') person. The other sphere of reference is a detail from Hardy's life; in conventional modes of analysis this would be seen as entirely dissociated from the former. The detail is his crass neglect of his first wife, and deplorable insensitivity towards his second. Tennant in an unprecedented fashion weighs them in the balance while estimating the sincerity of Hardy's sympathy for his fictional creation, Tess, and by extension, for all women.

While metafiction undoubtedly assists Tennant in reconciling the two, a second factor also comes to her aid. She is able to synthesise 'life' and 'text' in one framework, by integrating Hardy's life as it is recorded in a text. The text that Tennant uses for her purpose is Millgate's *Thomas Hardy: A Biography*. By interweaving biography and fiction, Tennant re-introduces intertextuality in its most apparent form of textual juxtaposition.

Tennant's novel begins with an aggressively pro-feminist tone, whose authority seems doubly entrenched on account of her biological gender; by the same token, Hardy's sets him at a disadvantage. The authors' respective genders are transferred to the narrators of the two novels. The narrator of *Tess of the d'Urbervilles* is probably Hardy himself while Liza-Lu, Tess's sister, recites *Tess*. Indeed her narration is an address to two listeners, Baby Tess and Ella. All three are women. Even little Ella is self-consciously female; already she is burdened with the consequences of being a girl in a man's world. In school, a male teacher has slapped her for her boisterousness, and this has subdued her personality in accordance with patriarchal requirements.

Ella also detests history, but Liza-Lu cannot over-emphasise the importance of learning this discipline. However, the history she has in mind is the alternative history of the distaff section of humanity. As a story of repression, this history has so far been suppressed by the male. The thrust of Liza-Lu's argument is this: 'How can I explain to you, Ella, that little girls can never be too careful? That there is danger everywhere, and no man can be trusted?' (Tennant 5).

By repulsing history Ella spurns the myth of male superiority and challenges its supposed impartiality of representation. In this attitude Tess Durbeyfield has quite appropriately set her a precedent. In Hardy's novel, Angel Clare offers to teach Tess history, but she expresses unwillingness to learn on the grounds that history is only another name for fatalism. This is especially the case with women, whose roles have been predetermined by men. Indeed Tess is brutally frank about the futility of Angel's efforts: ' "What's the use of learning that I am one of a long row only - finding out that there is set down in some old book somebody just like me, and to know that I shall only act her part; making me sad, that's all" ' (*Tess of the d'Urbervilles* 124). Tennant's version of Hardy's novel reveals itself as an elucidation of this statement. A repetition of Hardy's text is prefigured in the epigraph to her novel:

> Everything has already been lived and relived a thousand times by those who have disappeared but whom we carry in the very fibres of our being, just as we also carry in us the thousands of beings who will one day live after us. The only question, which incessantly poses itself, is why, of all these innumerable particles floating in each of us, certain ones come to the surface rather than others. (Tennant 1)

The epigraph reaffirms Hillis Miller's comment about the earlier *Tess*, *Tess of the d'Urbervilles*, that 'it is a story about repetition' (116). The difference is that Miller uncovers repetition as a textual pattern within Hardy's novel, while Tennant sees the entire novel as a replay of a patriarchal law. Her narrative repeats *Tess of the d'Urbervilles* with heavy irony, and the desire to end this repetition is also present in Tennant's enterprise. Although 'this story comes up again and again', 'now is the time it must end' (Tennant 5).

The ballad vouchsafes Tennant with an example of female authority, as we have pointed out in the chapter on this genre. Story-telling and female authorship were indivisible at one time in history. Hardy's stories were bequeathed to him by his mother (and were mostly about 'misalliance and mismating') (Tennant 125). Not only does this fact testify to the story-telling prerogative of the woman in the oral tradition; it more significantly shows the extent of Hardy's obligation to womanhood for his novels. This begs the question: how does Hardy acknowledge his inheritance? Tennant provides the sobering answer that Hardy has misappropriated the female imagination and furthermore done violence to it by making out of it a tale of rape and incest.

Her gender-prone narrative leads Tennant to describe the female act of narration through the metaphor of weaving. This metaphor is elaborated on in chapter two. The strikingly symbolic power of the loom amply conveys the seamless merging of womanhood and story-telling: 'the female side of the family tree is known as the distaff side because spinning was the work of women; and we must spin a new tapestry on our looms' (Tennant 50). By contrast male authorship, whether of a written text such as *Tess of the d'Urbervilles* or of an illegitimate child such as Tess Durbeyfield's, is a gesture of brutality that produces pain: 'Why it was that upon this beautiful feminine tissue, sensitive as gossamer, and practically blank as snow as yet, there should have been traced such a coarse pattern as it was doomed to receive;. . .' (*Tess of the d'Urbervilles* 71)[6]. What Hardy describes as unaesthetic and insensitive pertains not only to sexual imprints but to textual ones as well. What the male inscribes is crude and harsh; what the female records is artistic and beautiful. The former endures by virtue of force alone after erasing the latter.

The notion of destiny, which inexorably governs the plots of Hardy's novels, helps Tennant to imply an inevitability about feminism. There is a narrative inset in *Tess of the d'Urbervilles,* where Tess sees the portraits of her ancestresses (*Tess of the d'Urbervilles* 214). This provides a good example of the point I wish to make in this context. Tess is on her disastrous honeymoon in Wellbridge Manor, a short while before her confession to Angel Clare. Pausing on the landing of the stairs, she is momentarily discomfited by the disagreeable countenances of the d'Urberville ladies. A major reason for her sense of ill being is the unmistakable resemblance that her face bears to theirs (*Tess of the d'Urbervilles* 213–14).

Tennant resorts to the most direct kind of intertextuality, 'the quotation marks', in recalling this passage. *Tess* depicts Florence Hardy as recalling this textual extract from her husband's novel as she goes upstairs to her room, and here the parallel between Angel Clare's callousness and Hardy's insensitivity to their respective wives is drawn too strongly to be overlooked (Tennant 162–63). Tennant suggests through this example that if intertextuality implies a lineage, so does feminism. 'Hardy showed the portraits of those murderesses at Wellbridge (Wool Manor as it's taken to be) to Tess, to remind her that she would never be able to elude her destiny' (Tennant 164).

Fatality, incidentally, is also a major feature of ballad-narratives. Once again Tennant reminds her reader that the ballad genre is crucial to the feminist spirit of *Tess*. Ballads were sung before they came to be written, at a time when female authority over them was not disputed. Authorship was both anonymous and collective; imaginative re-telling was an act of aesthetic joy and not an area of contention, and intertextuality was the natural mode of artistic expression. The ballad was an inextricable part of the female mode of fathoming life: 'Like the tapestries, embroideries and patchworks which carried the message of our anonymous love or suffering, the oral tradition of telling stories was our great, unsigned charter' (Tennant 48). Tennant lays the blame on the Grimm brothers for looting this hoary tradition and defacing it by affixing their masculine signatures on this charter.

Her accusation creates a kind of intertextuality that links *Tess* with another Victorianist novel, *Possession*. Christabel LaMotte, the Victorian poetess of this novel, writes fairy tales like 'The Glass Coffin' which appear to originate from the Grimm brothers' stories, but which in fact predate all writing on account of their originally female proprietorship. The Grimms have raided the feminine store of narratives and (ab)used the stories to suit their masculine fancies. LaMotte rewrites the received version of 'Snow White and the Seven Dwarfs' which has all the makings of a masculine text, by effecting changes in its gender alliances. In the light of this, Tennant's sentence upon the Grimms produces the following intertextual alignments:

a) The brothers Grimm, by their act, foster a female bonding that manifests itself in a coincidental collusion between *Tess* and *Possession*, two Victorianist novels.
b) An intertextual link is achieved between the oral tradition as represented by the ballad and its female authorship.
c) A generic interconnection is forged and reinforced through gender, between the ballad and Tennant's novel *Tess*.

Tess of the d'Urbervilles, Thomas Hardy, and *Tess*

Unlike *Possession* or *FLW*, *Tess* engages with the issue of gender by dialoguing with only one Victorian novel, which its title suffices to indicate. Analysis of the intertextual mechanism of *Tess* relies heavily on a gender-based review of Thomas Hardy's *Tess of the d'Urbervilles*. The consensual verdict on Hardy's novel has been that it supports the incipient feminism of the Victorians to perhaps unseemly extremes. Seymour-Smith observes of Hardy's espousal of the feminist cause that 'A few dissenting voices. . . apart, he had won a considerable victory' (Seymour-Smith 426). In her book on the sexuality of Hardy's heroines, Rosemarie Morgan identifies some of these voices: 'Hardy sets at odds those *social and literary conventions* which mutually reinforced the culturally based induction, in Victorian England, of a sexual "amnesia" in women' (Morgan x–xi, emphasis mine).

Seymour-Smith points out that Hardy developed the character of Tess from a common Victorian stereotype: the ruined maid (429). For Tennant this seems providential; the scene seems to be set for the production of a Victorianist novel, as a powerful Victorian stereotype is already at hand for re-vision. However, Hardy's treatment of the ruined maid is anything but stereotypical. He took a different path when he transcended the Victorian dichotomous representation of woman as 'angel/monster', and adapted the stereotype of the seduced innocent to show that she could still be pure. In such a character as

Tess, Hardy reconciled sexuality with morality, which were defined antithetically by the Victorians. For this, he was 'charged with misrepresenting womankind' (Morgan xiv).

The truth is that Hardy was himself reacting to representations of womanhood as prevalent in contemporary stereotypes of the 'angel in the house' and 'stainless sceptre of womanhood', popularised by Coventry Patmore and Ruskin respectively (Morgan xiv). Tess's sexual voluptuousness disturbed the Victorians, and such a description as the following would in all likelihood deeply offend if not enrage: 'yet there was nothing ethereal about it, all was real vitality, real warmth, real incarnation. And it was in her mouth that this culminated. . . . To a young man with the least fire in him that little upward lift in the middle of her red top lip was distracting, infatuating, maddening' (*Tess of the d'Urbervilles* 147–48).

In this and like manner, Hardy appears to have preempted Tennant in his ardent defence of womanhood and her sexuality. In the light of *Tess of the d'Urbervilles* Tennant's labour seems superfluous; nevertheless she turns the tables entirely on Hardy by rejecting what for her would be a stereotype, namely the received notion of Hardy as a feminist. A problem for Tennant lies in the fact that twentieth-century interpretations of *Tess of the d'Urbervilles*, no less than Victorian ones, increasingly view Hardy as a feminist rather than chauvinist or voyeur. The Victorianism of Tennant's enterprise requires her to address both centuries in their appreciation of *Tess of the d'Urbervilles*. Her address takes the form of an attack, and she fortifies her position by relying on texts outside Hardy's novel for sustenance. One of these is the feminist tradition. In a passage replete with irony, Tennant's narrator Liza-Lu compares Tess with Eve:

> She tempted Adam. . . . She remains on earth to tempt men (remember Hardy's Tess, who is told strictly by the apparently reformed New Man and preacher Alex d'Urberville after her abandonment by Angel, the only man she could love, that she must on no account 'tempt' him: this after his seduction and subsequent refusal to take responsibility for the baby that was the consequence of it!) For all Hardy's apparent compassion for Tess and his description of her on the title page of the book that became him, overcame him and stayed more in the imagination of the world than anything else of him–as a 'Pure Woman', he was as guilty as the next man. His compassion was an exquisite cruelty. . . he shaped her, through all the ages of history that woman has toiled, died in the agony of labour, stood at the stake, fallen gagging on black water in the duck ponds of witch persecution – through all the centuries of slavery and non-belonging, without even a name or a woman priest to turn to in the hours of worst desolation, Hardy led Tess to the last,

> inevitable punishment, the price she must pay as daughter of Eve. For her prime disobedience to man, her ruler, her father, her seducer, Tess must swing. (Tennant 82)

Feminist declamations such as these reverberate across the novel. Towards the beginning, *Tess* celebrates a saint, whose feminism is resistant to masculine inroads, even if they took the legal form of matrimony. This is St Catherine, of whom Liza-Lu speaks with reverential awe as the patron saint of spinsters; adding that unmarried women deserved neither derision nor sympathy, but admiration for their independence. Spinsters belonged to the first all-women guilds in medieval times; they had complete control over their wealth, which they acquired by selling lace and linen handkerchiefs (Tennant 13). Their methods of self-sufficiency were also aesthetic: they wove, they stitched, and they embroidered, in much the same manner as their sisters told stories.

The second text that Tennant draws substantially upon is biography. Unlike the pervasive tenor of feminism that lies dispersed through *Tess*, the biographical text is specific, and is responsible for the details about Hardy's marital life. The very phrases are repeated from Millgate's biography and are suitably modified by Tennant to frame Hardy as guilty.

Comparisons between specific, corresponding sections of Millgate's *Thomas Hardy* and Tennant's *Tess* reveal that innocuously recorded facts become divested of their innocence in the latter, so that they may be used to condemn Hardy. The reader cannot but wonder whether Millgate's account glosses over Hardy's sins both of commission and omission, or if Tennant imputes a heartlessness to Hardy that he really did not possess? For instance, there is Millgate's report of Emma Hardy's withdrawal into the attic in Max Gate; he describes the process as the culmination of a period during which Emma openly criticised her husband, increasingly neglecting him for an active social life (Millgate 355). When it is Tennant's turn to report this episode, she seizes upon the famous description of Bertha Mason by Gilbert and Gubar: 'Yes, Thomas Hardy made of his wife that well-known Victorian phenomenon, *the madwoman in the attic*' (Tennant 127, emphasis mine). Tennant does not refer to Emma's spirited independence. In her version, Emma is a passive victim of her husband's whims.

It is possible to infer that Millgate tackles this question with greater impartiality than Tennant. He regards both Emma and Hardy as victims of an unhappy marriage, but nevertheless concedes of Emma that 'it is impossible to ignore the almost universal contemporary impression of her as opinionated, inconsequential, vain, tiresome, and often downright disagreeable' (Millgate 398). Millgate admits, 'Hardy could certainly have treated her with more kindness and consideration' (482), although it is not necessary 'to judge him more harshly than he did himself' (Millgate 480–81). But Tennant remains inexorable in her one-sided view of the marriage as cruel and unfair to Emma.

The two radically different textual accounts, Millgate's biography and Tennant's novel, converge over the same detail to present it in polarised terms; when Emma moves to the attic rooms she tells Rebekah Owen, 'My boudoir is my sweet refuge and solace – not a sound scarcely penetrates hither. I see the sun, & [sic] stars and moon rise & [sic] the birds come to my bird table when a hurricane has not sent it flying' (Millgate 391). Tennant reinterprets this passage to cast it in a feminist light as follows: 'There, in the attic room, where the birds, with whom Emma had an almost magical rapport, flock to the window and look in at their ill protector – here, in the bed Hardy had left unvisited for as long as anyone can remember, poor 'mad' Emma dies' (Tennant 127). The comparatively impersonal account of Emma's loneliness that the previous passage provides is transformed into a feminist text by the emphasis on Emma's illness that draws attention to her neglected state. An explicit plea is made for sympathy by the use of the epithet 'poor'. The use of quotation marks for 'mad' could suggest that a hard-hearted husband drove Emma to madness just as Bertha was, in *WSS*.

Such descriptions as the following add to the impartial tone of Millgate's text. Emma was attended by a maid called Dolly who waited on her through day and night. Yet Emma took care never to disturb her during the night, lest her sleep be broken: thus Millgate shows himself capable of representing Emma as considerate, as well as unlovable. Tennant, on the other hand, takes the extreme stance of depicting Hardy as a villain. She can neither exonerate him nor dilute his vices, let alone present him objectively.

Her task is made easier because of such observations made by Millgate himself. When Dolly is shaken by Emma's death throes she goes to Hardy. Here she had 'difficulty in persuading him of the seriousness of the situation. . . when he did follow her back up the stairs – no doubt the first time he had climbed them in many months – he found Emma already far too gone to speak' (Millgate 485). Taking her cue from here, Tennant does not stint on the pathos surrounding Emma's death in *Tess* (127).

In general a dichotomy prevails over the respective textual accounts of Hardy's personal life in *Thomas Hardy* and *Tess*: the former seems less biased against Hardy and the latter very much more so. This difference continues in the descriptions of Florence Hardy's heartache and her silent sufferings, while Hardy, all of a sudden, begins to eulogise over his dead wife Emma, whom he had disregarded in her lifetime, and simultaneously develops a *tendre* for Gertrude Bugler. To enhance the veracity of her story, Tennant also introduces excerpts from Sir Sydney Cockerell's diary, which notes Florence's unhappiness in no uncertain terms (Tennant 178). The entry for '11th January 1925' has a near-exact parallel in Millgate (557), so that Tennant's version seems to be twice ratified by (two different) external texts. Tennant herein produces a facsimile replication of Millgate:

> Gertrude Bugler never forgave Florence for denying the chance of appearing in the West End in 1925. When, with Florence's active encouragement, she did at last play Tess in London after Hardy's death, she felt that she was already too old to embark upon a professional career as a romantic actress. (Tennant 180, Millgate 557–58)

In this last example, *Tess* holds a powerful subtext that is missing in Millgate's monotonic report. The import of these words is markedly feminist; Hardy is condemned for breaking female sisterhood and causing a breach between two women, whose common sex and gender-affiliations should have brought them together. Tennant's intertextual method here is the same as Menard's in rewriting *Quixote*, producing a sophisticated echoic utterance that is identical on the surface so that the difference is harder to detect.

Notwithstanding this torrent of feminist artillery upon *Tess of the d'Urbervilles* and its author, it is imperative for a Victorianist writer to question if Hardy was being as feminist in his novel as the uncompromising Victorian ethos would allow. The reply seems an unambiguous affirmative. At every stage in Hardy's novel Tess's suffering is represented as being visited upon her by a male. Her father's propensity for vanity and irresponsibility, Alec's dishonourable intentions, Angel's double standards, and even the Vicar's harshness in refusing to baptise her baby, all have their role in ruining Tess. The men in her life desert Tess after exploiting her. In the light of the belief that a novel has certain obligations towards verisimilitude, could Hardy have created a Tess who could murder Alec and get away from the reach of the law? If he had written such a novel its feminist purpose would have dissipated, and his narrative dismissed as a fantasy.

Without contesting Tennant's right to consider Hardy's personal depravity in estimating his novel, it must be acknowledged that Tennant's crusading has an excess of fervour that can jeopardise her novel. A pressing question that Tennant does not ever raise is: does Alec seduce Tess, or does he rape her?[7] This is a much-discussed area in critical reviews of *Tess of the d'Urbervilles.* The question, no less than the answer, is fundamental to a gender-biased rewriting of *Tess of the d'Urbervilles*.

Tennant quotes directly from Hardy's novel in her eight descriptions of Tess's enchanting mouth (Tennant 57, *Tess of the d'Urbervilles* 8, 9, 49, 89, 148, 166). The Alecs and the Angels were aware of it; but then, so was Tess herself as Hardy depicts in her dalliance with Angel. Tennant's Tess, too, when caught with Alec by her father John Hewitt, shows no sign of distress or indication that Alec has forced her into a sexual act. Her sexual encounter with Alec is one of mutual consent rather than rape.

Undoubtedly *Tess* is stylistically rich because of its intertextual foundation, even though its gender-assumptions appear to be less well-founded in their unadulterated assault on Thomas Hardy. Tennant's ingenuity leads her to repeat the story of Tess Durbeyfield within a twentieth-century context. Her protagonist is a 'modern' Tess of the 1950s in Dorset with a boyfriend called Alec. She has a sexual relationship with him, and later falls in love with Gabriel (the modern 'Angel') through whom she has a child. Unlike Tess Durbeyfield's son who dies as an infant, this child is a daughter who survives. Soon after, Gabriel deserts Tess who has no Alec to support her now.

On this intertextual basis, Tennant richly develops other cross-textual threads. She introduces a visual signifier in the dramatic productions of *Tess of the d'Urbervilles*. This gives her a platform to examine such pivots of intertextuality, as reality, illusion, and fictionalising techniques. Here is an account of the rehearsal of the play:

> We have to laugh when we contrast the terrible, dark and tragic scene that Thomas Hardy painted of that honeymoon at Wool Manor - when his Tess, seduced by Alec d'Urberville, mother of his (now-dead) child trusts and confides her secret to Angel, thus losing him for ever - with the reality of the rehearsal. Poor Gertrude! Alone there with the foolish old bard and a balding Dr E. W. Smerdon as Angel Clare.
>
> (Tennant 158)

By focussing spotlight on the illusory nature of the play, Tennant invests *Tess* with metafictional potential.

Tess accrues further potential for debate in the light of a parallel Victorianist novel, which is John Fowles's *FLW*. In Morgan's opinion, Hardy adopted an anti-Victorian stance in dissociating female sexuality from matrimony (Rosemarie Morgan xv). In Hardy's view sexuality, even for a woman, did not need a social bind to justify or fulfil itself. This thesis is brought to fruition in the character of Sarah in *FLW*. In a glaring reversal of gender-roles, Sarah deceives Charles into seducing her by pretending that she is not a virgin, which she actually is, as he discovers after the event. Charles is even more anxious to marry her upon this discovery than before but despite (or perhaps because of) this, Sarah will not marry him. Sarah's decision would have received Hardy's stamp of approval, who was at least a century ahead of Victorian thinking in matters pertaining to woman's sexual independence.

WSS: The Breach in *Jane Eyre*

When Matthew Arnold wrote of Charlotte Brontë that her 'mind contains nothing but hunger, rebellion, and rage' (quoted in Gilbert and Gubar 337), he was echoing the opinion of his age about *Jane Eyre*. This novel upset existing parameters of acceptable behaviour in a woman as well as the decorum with which a love affair between the sexes must proceed; in short, the narrative boiled down to 'rebellious feminism' (Gilbert and Gubar 338). The text is full of Jane's anger, an emotion that enables her to survive experiences of deprivation and humiliation, for which the usual Victorian prescription would have been docile submission.

The feminist principles of Jane, the protagonist/heroine, are largely responsible for the gender-orientation of *Jane Eyre*. The mutual attraction between Jane and Rochester engenders the conflicts that punctuate the narrative, and the kind of overt sexual representation that this novel offers may well have offended prudish Victorian sensibilities. However, more crucial to the gender-semantics of the novel is the opposition between Jane and Bertha, the mad first wife of Rochester, and thus already a rival to Jane.

It is this arraying of characters that Jean Rhys turns to her advantage in her own novel, *Wide Sargasso Sea*. By placing Jane and Bertha against each other, *Jane Eyre* generates a division of loyalty in feminist terms, a division that Rhys is quick to perceive and explore. Jane can defend her own rights on the basis of her womanhood, but her inability to sympathise with Bertha and indeed her noticeable lack of compassion for her is too glaring to pass notice. Rarely if ever, does Jane consider the injustice that Bertha has suffered at Rochester's hands. This fact dissipates the feminist impulse of *Jane Eyre* beyond doubt. When Rochester importunes Jane to be his mistress, much as she desires to succumb she resists the impulse with this self-admonition: 'I care for myself. The more solitary, the more friendless, the more unsustained I am, the more I will respect myself' (*Jane Eyre* 314). Yet her respect, even empathy, falls short of reaching Bertha, who is also solitary, friendless and unsustained.

Classic feminist interpretations of *Jane Eyre* such as Gilbert and Gubar's suggestively entitled *The Madwoman in the Attic*, transcend this textual impediment by proposing that Jane and Bertha are two diametrically opposed halves of the same self (Gilbert and Gubar 359)[8]. They propound the thesis that Thornfield is a metaphor for Jane's own life. The third story is the most obviously emblematic quarter of Thornfield (Gilbert and Gubar 347–48), since Bertha is immured on this floor of the house. The feminist thrust of their interpretation is built on the notion that Bertha is not only 'Rochester's secret wife' but also 'in a sense her own secret self' (Gilbert and Gubar 348). As for their interpretation of Jane's feelings for Rochester, she 'begins to fall in love with him not because he is her master but in spite of the fact that he is, not because he is princely in manner, but. . . in some sense her equal' (Gilbert and Gubar 352).

Jean Rhys remains impervious to such allegorical re-visions and obdurately adheres to a straightforward, if literal, reading of the Jane–Bertha encounters. Rhys sees an innate racism in Jane that she cannot forgive, were a moral judgement to be invoked. According to Rhys, Jane's own sidelined status arising from factors including poverty, social background and her sex, ought to have made her more sensitive to Bertha's plight. Right at the beginning, *Jane Eyre* shows Jane's exclusion from her cousins' company, and the experience of ostracism comes to repeat itself with remarkable regularity throughout her life; hence her blindness to Bertha's predicament becomes doubly puzzling.

Inherent in *WSS* is the premise that arguments involving gender include 'race'. In this manner, Rhys finds in the experience of ostracism a bond between gender and racial concerns. Brontë's novel underscores the association between Bertha's madness and her West Indian upbringing as though the latter were a cause of the former (Thorpe 101). Rhys ruthlessly brings this racial undercurrent in *Jane Eyre* to light in *WSS*. She advances the notion that a bias in favour of women, a marginalised section of humanity, is undercut in *Jane Eyre*, by a bias against a coloured human being, a Creole and also a marginalised section of humanity. Thereby Rhys also provides a reading of *Jane Eyre* as superficially feminist.

Wide Sargasso Sea

Despite projecting a feminist ideal more stringent than that of *Jane Eyre*, *WSS* conveys the impression of a balance in outlook. This is partly an effect of its structure. Unlike *Jane Eyre* which is narrated solely by Jane, *WSS* is divided into three sections. The first and the third are Bertha's narratives in the first person mode and they frame Rochester's monologue, which comprises the second part. These breaks in perspective are responsible for more than one point of view and indeed, for a counterpoint of view in terms of gender. They also bring the novel closer to *Jane Eyre* by having a major character of Brontë's creation speak in his voice – a privilege that even Brontë does not afford him. The implied irony here is that despite being authored by a woman, the feminism of *Jane Eyre* cannot measure up to that of its Victorianist complement. There are breaches in its feminist thesis that require to be filled.

In its conception, *WSS* is poised on more than one type of gender-initiated intertextuality: a) interaction between a Victorian feminist text and a Victorianist feminist one, b) interaction between two texts authored by women; and c) interaction between gender and race.

The most significant intertextual achievement of *WSS* is feminist in an indisputable sense, consisting of a shift in reader-response from horror and revulsion for the female character Bertha, to sympathy and indignation for her. The seeds of Rhys's narrative are contained in a remark made by Charlotte *Brontë* herself: 'It is true that profound pity ought to be the only sentiment elicited by the view of such degradation (as Bertha's) and equally true is it that I have not sufficiently dwelt on that feeling: I have erred in making *horror* too predominant' (quoted in Thorpe 101). The feminist dynamics of *Jane Eyre* is also toned down by the compassion that the reader is forced to feel for Rochester (a male), who has suffered at the hands of Bertha (a female). Clearly, racial prejudice limits the reach of Brontë's pity which can envelop Jane but unfeelingly overlook Bertha (Thorpe 105).

WSS can probably be read as an independent, coherent text, but there is no doubt that its import will suffer if read independently of *Jane Eyre*. Unlike *Possession* or *FLW* whose Victorianism is a consequence of representing generic or ideological Victorian-like features, *WSS* (like *Tess*) derives from a specific Victorian text. To neglect this aspect is to ignore the complex network of chronology that *WSS* manipulates, which precludes it from being a simple sequel. To take an instance, though written much later, *WSS* boasts knowledge of events that 'happened' prior to those in *Jane Eyre*[9]. This apart, the reader has to remember at least four time-frames and dates: a) 1847, the date of publication of *Jane Eyre*; b) The period when the events forming the narrative of *Jane Eyre* are supposed to take place; c) 1966, when *WSS* was first published, and d) The historical period its events ostensibly belong to.

The reader is moreover required to remember the intriguing relationship between these four time-units to appreciate the sophistication of its intertextual identity. The historical context of *WSS* reveals another kind of biased ideology (besides that pertaining to gender) which existed in the Victorian period, and which is unwittingly revealed in the plot-mechanism of *Jane Eyre*: colonialism. Bertha is a white Creole and belongs to a non-privileged social class, which goes a long way towards divesting her of sympathy from her author and the readership the author is addressing.

Intertextual Intersections

Certain motifs repeat themselves in *WSS*, which have their origin in *Jane Eyre*. One is the dream. Jane herself has vivid dreams, some of which are in the nature of premonitions. One is a vision of Thornfield as 'a dreary ruin, the retreat of bats and owls' (*Jane Eyre* 279). Later, at the end of her exhaustive adventures and after her telepathic communication with Rochester, when Jane returns to Thornfield she 'looked with timorous joy towards a stately house', only to find it 'a blackened ruin', as she had dreamed it (*Jane Eyre* 423).

There are other textual junctions such as Bertha's glimpse of Jane, or her attack on Richard Mason. In Rhys's initial evocation of *Jane Eyre*, Jane is first described by Bertha. Bertha does not know the name of the girl she is describing, but we, the readers of *Jane Eyre,* have no trouble in identifying Jane.

> Turning a corner I saw a girl coming out of her bedroom. She wore a white dress and she was humming to herself. I flattened myself against the wall for I did not wish her to see me, but she stopped and looked around. She saw nothing but shadows, I took care of that, but she didn't walk to the head of the stairs. She ran. She met another girl and the second girl said, 'Have you seen a ghost?' (*WSS* 149)

Bertha's assault upon Richard Mason finds description in both *Jane Eyre* and *WSS*. In the former novel Jane describes the episode (*Jane Eyre,* 206–9), while in the latter, Grace Poole narrates this violent incident to Bertha thus: 'This gentleman arrived suddenly and insisted on seeing you and that was all the thanks he got. You rushed at him with a knife and when he got the knife away you bit his arm' (*WSS* 150). Let us compare it with the original. In *Jane Eyre* the information conveyed by Richard is that 'She bit me', and 'worried me like a tigress, when Rochester got the knife from her'. Although the details appear to be the same, the implication of Richard's communication is that Rochester took the knife away from Bertha, while the ambiguously represented version in *WSS* encourages the deduction that Richard himself removed the knife. We can speculate on the reason for this change in Rhys's version; one possibility that presents itself is that Rochester is divested of whatever 'courage' and 'heroism' he may have thought to possess in taking the knife away from a mad woman.

Intersections between *Jane Eyre* and *WSS* in respect of characterisation offer themselves to a rewarding analysis. The genius of Jean Rhys rests in the way she secures the reader's compassion for Bertha without maligning Rochester. Here *WSS* markedly deviates from the intertextual strategy of a Victorianist novel like *Tess*. Rochester, as Rhys delineates him, is harsh and unyielding; but his honesty redeems him. He admits frankly that he was never in love with Bertha, and was tricked into marrying her (*Jane Eyre* 303, *WSS* 132–33). His father and brother had both known of the madness in Bertha's family, but cupidity had made them acquiesce in the wedding arrangement. Therefore, Rochester is as much a victim as Bertha. Rhys's forte lies in retaining this view in her retold version of the story, without jeopardising the reader's sympathy for Bertha. By coaxing an alternative reader-response for Bertha from virtually the same text, Jean Rhys shows how *Jane Eyre* internally sabotages itself.

WSS describes Bertha's marriage in feminist terms: she is 'sexually exploited for a time, and when once she has grown dependent on his love and his lovemaking, rejected. . .' (Porter 543). Rhys also castigates Charlotte Brontë for her sexual double-standard and ethic which translates a sexually experienced man as 'virile' and his female counterpart as 'unchaste'. Jane, although aware of her sexuality, is inexperienced and this combination fascinates Rochester. He is unapologetic about his own experience but denounces Bertha for hers as 'at once intemperate and unchaste'[10] (*Jane Eyre* 304).

Names have an important role to play in establishing identity. Rochester chooses to rename 'Bertha' as 'Antoinette' in Rhys's novel, and this is one of the significant ways in which he asserts his power over her. But he cannot wield such authority over Jane. After ten years of marriage, Jane writes the story of her life under the title 'Jane Eyre' and not 'Mrs Rochester'. Indeed it is Rochester who 'becomes' 'Edward' in Jane's narrative (Porter 550). The same device used by Charlotte Brontë to affirm her heroine's independence is intertextually recalled and refashioned by Jean Rhys to suit her feminist aim of portraying a helpless heroine.

Other Novels

Gender exists incontrovertibly as a line of inquiry for the careful reader in other Victorianist novels as well. The title of Fowles's novel is sufficiently indicative of the heroine's importance over the hero's; indeed Sarah is the 'hero' of the novel. Fowles pays her a great tribute when, at the end of a narrative spanning four hundred pages but one, he grants her the right to reject Charles. This is a remarkable reversal of roles where a socially condemned Victorian woman, assumes control in a sexual relationship. Victorian gender-politics firmly forbade such a configuration. As Charles reflects at one point, he 'had known women – frequently Ernestina herself – contradict him playfully. But that was in a playful context. A woman did not contradict a man's opinion when he was being serious unless it were in carefully measured terms' (*FLW* 124).

Fowles breaks the mould as well as the gender code of the Victorians by introducing Sarah Woodruff, who is mysterious, unpredictable and unfathomable. Furthermore, Fowles respects these qualities in her, and one of the ways in which he shows his respect is by refusing to violate her mind, and not interfering in any way with her independence. She who is introduced as a Sphinx at the beginning of the novel, remains one until the end, giving substance to the title of the first epigraph from Hardy's poem, 'The Riddle' (*FLW* 7).

Fowles's familiarity with gender-related tensions in the Victorian sociological landscape reveals itself in the document that he produces midway in the novel, thus creating an intertextual event (*FLW* 199–204). This contains a record of the trial of Lieutenant Emile de La Ronciere in 1835, which Dr Grogan gives Charles to read in the hope that it may explain the strange ways of Sarah. The trial graphically narrates the mental and psychological aberrations that a woman was popularly supposed to suffer during her menstrual phases. While this text appears to explain a similar irrationality in Sarah's subsequent behaviour with Charles, the novel unfolds to show that Sarah's deviant behaviour is a result of possessing a mind that is extremely modern, and not any biological/physiological reasons.

Even Charles understands the full import of his encounter with Sarah only towards the end of the novel. Earlier, when he realises that he has forced a virgin and that Sarah has had no prior sexual experience whatsoever, his reaction is one of intense shock. Gripped by terror, his mind envisages various possibilities for her unusual conduct. They are all base, including even blackmail:

> And all those loathsome succubi of the male mind, their fat fears of a great feminine conspiracy to suck the virility from their veins, to prey upon their idealism, melt them into wax and mould them to their evil fancies... these, and a surging back to credibility of the hideous evidence adduced in the La Ronciere appeal, filled Charles's mind with an apocalyptic horror. (*FLW* 307–8)

For the narrator of 'Morpho Eugenia' (*Angels and Insects*), the feminist position is espoused by Mother Nature herself who gives precedence to the female. A study of mating behaviour among insects discloses all amatory overtures to be made by the male, who aspires to fulfil the female's demands in every respect. Studying the butterflies, Adamson explains that the males 'dress' up, 'making themselves brilliant for their brown mates. The Indians resemble them in that. It is the men who dress in brilliant feathers and coloured paint and stones. The females are quieter' (*Angels and Insects* 7). He compares the 'civilised' world of Victorian England unfavourably with the primitive societies of the Amazon. 'Whereas here we men wear carapaces like black beetles. And you ladies are like a flower garden in full flight' (*Angels and Insects* 7). This novella also features a passage on the greatly indulged Queen Ant whose position of preeminence is analogous to that of the Queen Bee (37). It implicitly mocks the Victorian social system, which denigrates women, and Victorian attitudes to gender relations are judged in 'Morpho Eugenia' as unnatural.

This survey of gender and textuality in Victorianist novels culminates in the following observations. First, Victorianist novels like *Tess* and *WSS* that take inspiration from a specific Victorian text demonstrate the way in which gender-consciousness intensifies their intertextual machinery. Even independent novels like *FLW* tacitly acknowledge the impossibility of presenting a Victorian milieu without speaking of gender. Fowles indicates several times that he is rewriting as well as re-'right'ing an entrenched gender-prejudice of Victorian culture and textuality, by granting Sarah the power to dismiss Charles from her life. It is tempting to liken Fowles's feminist agenda with that of Thomas Hardy, the Victorian writer he so admires; but to do so would set another intertextual dialogue in motion with *Tess*.

While considering gender and intertextuality in Victorianist novels, it is important to give weight to Gilbert and Gubar's statement that nineteenth-century texts by women were written as a response either to male texts or to male perceptions and depictions of females (Gilbert and Gulbar xi–xii). In this sense, gender in texts occupies an 'already' intertextual role. When women writers first asserted their presence as a sizeable community in the nineteenth century, they had to battle against a male-structured literary lineage. A prior tradition of texts moulded by gendered authority, opposed their literary endeavours. Women writers were seen as presumptuous invaders into a hostile territory.

Yet their tenacity won the day for them–or rather the age, as the nineteenth century is described as the period of the woman novelist[11]. Viewed from this angle, the Victorianist novel becomes compulsorily intertextual. Gender is naturally woven into Victorianism. By concerning itself with the nineteenth century, the Victorianist novel has no choice but to recognise gender as the keynote of Victorian social, intellectual and literary debate.

Notes

1 Rukmini Bhaya Nair makes the observation that there is a linguistic nexus between studies of gender, genre and generative grammar. For one, they have a common etymological origin in 'genesis'. 'Gender, genre, and generative grammar: Deconstructing the matrimonial column'. *Language, Text and Context: Essays in Stylistics* ed. Michael Toolan (London and New York: Routledge, 1992) 227–54.

2 'One of the first feminist projects was to examine portrayals of female characters in male-authored texts (de Beauvoir 1952; Ellmann 1968; Millett 1969). Finding abundant evidence of misogyny in these characters and in gender characterisations in general, many feminist critics were persuaded that male authors could not speak truly about women. Consequently, they proposed that whatever one could consider as a female presence in male-authored text would necessarily be filtered through the complex workings of male desire'. 'Notorious signs, feminist criticism and literary tradition' by Adrienne Munich, in *Making a Difference: Feminist Literary Criticism*, ed. Gayle Greene and Coppelia Kahn (London: Routledge, 1985) 242.

3 For a brilliant unravelling of these features, see Sandra M. Gilbert and Susan Gubar, *The Madwoman in the Attic* (New Haven: Yale University Press, 1979) 36–43.

4 The Sphinx operates cross-textually between the Victorianist novels. Sarah is called a Sphinx, too. John Fowles, *FLW* (London: Pan Books, 1987) 399.

5 Though Ash's dramatic monologue blatantly discredits the female medium, Hella Lees appears to be genuine. Her autobiography does not disclose spurious means of conducting séances. There is also a supposedly neutral text by Miss Olivia Judge which verifies Hella Lees as an authentic medium. A. S. Byatt, *Possession: A Romance* (London: Vintage, 1990) 396–97.

6 Hardy's metaphor for the sexual act takes the reader to Isak Dinesen's short story, 'The Blank Page' told by an old woman, who learned the art of storytelling from her grandmother, who in turn learned it from *her* grandmother. It is the story of nuns in a convent who grow, spin and weave bridal sheets for the princesses of the royal house. After the wedding night, these sheets, now bloodstained, are displayed on the balcony of the palace. While Dinesen takes the story onwards to prove a feminist point about patriarchal fears of female sexuality and the male desire to control it, the metaphor of the story thus far is similar to Hardy's comparison between the writing on a page and the way in which the sexual act is defined between the male and the female (from *Making a Difference: Feminist Literary Criticism* ed. Gayle Greene and Coppelia Kahn, New York: Routledge, 1985, 5–6).

7 Gender-oriented implications of the scene in *Tess of the d'Urbervilles* where Alec waylays Tess, were debated on list Victoria, an electronic mail study group, during the first week of April 1996. Richard Nemesvari believes that owing to contradictory statements after the event, the text generates indeterminacy of meaning. As Keith Wilson perceptively remarks, Tess is not only physically vulnerable but also economically, emotionally and

psychologically so. His other observation is related to the way that textual modes and media influence each other. 'The exclusive and largely unexamined rape assumption began to dominate at around the same time as the release of the Roman Polanski film of Tess, the advertising posters for which. . . made the act unequivocally a rape.' Interpretations that are explicitly feminist would tend to assume that Alec raped Tess, and construct their argument on this basis.

8 Elaine Showalter also speaks of Bertha as a symbolic alter-ego of Jane in *A Literature of Their Own* (London: Virago Press Ltd., 1982) 113–22.

9 Here Rhys pretends that narrative events have a historical reality. A novel with a similar structural positioning as *Wide Sargasso Sea* but without a twentieth-century perspective is Eleanor Thomson's *A Time Before Oliver* (London: Harper Collins, 1996) which moves backwards from the story of *Oliver Twist* to provide the reasons that drove Bill Sikes and Nancy to crime. Thomson calls her novel a 'prequel' to *Oliver Twist*, without, however, probing the implications of a sequel 'in reverse'. Her novel exhibits no self-awareness.

10 Showalter echoes a Victorian attitude when she notes that 'sexual appetite was considered one of the chief symptoms of moral insanity in women', in *A Literature of Their Own* (London: Virago Press Ltd., 1982) 120.

11 To mention just the most famous, Charlotte Brontë, Emily Brontë, Anne Brontë, Mrs Gaskell and George Eliot.

5 Intertextual Devices

In the foregoing chapters we have seen the ways in which genre can promote intertextuality. Besides full-fledged genres, there are also minor texts that participate in the creation of an intertextual happening. This chapter catalogues these textual devices and assesses their potential in carrying intertextual proceedings through.

As pointed out earlier, one of the most common guises in which intertextuality garbs itself is that of textual juxtaposition. When the text is uni-generic (as most texts are), the reader stands every chance of losing himself to the text. However, two genres, when placed next to each other, or within each other, create a fissure in the spatial configuration of the larger text. A host of smaller texts such as the letter, the footnote, and the epigraph, when embedded in a larger genre or juxtaposed alongside it, also work towards a similar result. These smaller texts become highly effective devices in carving intertextual identity. Such texts proliferate in *Possession*, *FLW*, and *Tess*, but particularly so in the first example.

The Title

By virtue of their position in the forefront, titles make strategic intertextual texts. Thus Emma Tennant confidently entitles her novel 'Tess', which despite its brevity effortlessly recalls Hardy's *Tess of the d'Urbervilles*. The connection between the two texts is established right at the outset by their titles. Thereafter Tennant assumes a literary audience and takes for granted the reader's ability to make other intertextual associations. The intertextual challenge lies in the author's capacity to make changes even while retaining the original character of the narrative, and Tennant does take her narrative forward, beyond the boundaries of its *ur*-text. Her ambitiously intertextual *Tess* works against some of the expectations imposed by its title, in order to exceed the scope of its source-novel and enlarge it in some way. This is part of a prior understanding between the reader and the writer of an intertextual work, that while drawing upon a former text, the author of the present text dilate upon his source in some significant manner. *Tess* rests on this understanding, and its reader finds himself urged towards a reconsideration of a hitherto staunchly held opinion of Thomas Hardy as a feminist writer, particularly in *Tess of the d'Urbervilles*.

Unlike other Victorianist novels like *Possession* and *Heathcliff*, for instance,[1] *Tess* is marked by the absence of a subtitle. This may seem like rather a grave omission in the light of Hardy's provocative subtitle to his *Tess of the d'Urbervilles*: 'A Pure Woman'. Millgate points out that Hardy incorporated this subtitle 'after his final reading of the proofs "as being the estimate left in a candid mind of the heroine's character"; it was also a deliberate challenge' (Millgate 318–19).

'Tess' is nothing if not bold in its undeclared assumption that in itself it is more than adequate to impel the reader to make intertextual connections. In a strange reversal of the chronological norm, it is the earlier title that appears to need a qualification: Hardy's title is longer than Tennant's; he seemed to have found the need to specify his heroine's lineage as well as establish her character. When Tennant dispenses with the subtitle she indicates among other things, that her text universalises the hitherto Victorian phenomenon called 'Tess'.

An echoing title of this kind operates on the principle of optimal relevance advanced by Sperber and Wilson, and is useful for understanding intertextuality. 'A speaker aiming at optimal relevance will leave implicit everything her hearer can be trusted to supply with less effort than would be needed to process an explicit prompt' (Sperber and Wilson 218). A text is optimally relevant when it supplies as little information as possible without endangering its intelligibility. 'Tess' is a name that suggests Hardy and Victorian literature – to the knowledgeable reader. As such, it is an optimally relevant device.

The role of subtitles is similar to titles. An intertextual subtitle of a slightly different nature from Hardy's is *Possession: A Romance*. Unlike the former, which describes the protagonist, Byatt's subtitle directs the reader towards viewing the text in a specific generic perspective. Here the expectations of the reader are directed towards the general features of the plot, rather than the particular course taken by the story. Mystery is one of the main features of the romance; and on the most fundamental level the entire story of *Possession* hinges on uncovering the mysterious lives of Ash, Ellen and Christabel. As a final tribute to the triumph of mystery, Byatt uses her authorial omniscience to share one last secret with the reader, and this story of the meeting between Ash and his daughter is told only to the reader. Other characters in the text are kept in ignorance.

The Proper Name

Quite like titles, names too function as markers. They link texts with each other or with historical figures belonging to a particular period:

in this case, the Victorian. In *Possession*, three names that are directly and obliquely related to the Victorian literary ethos are 'Ash', 'Christabel' and 'Maud'. Ash helpfully makes a self-conscious reference to his name by evoking mythology and then citing Tennyson as an added support. 'The mighty Ash. . . is a common and magical tree – not as the mountain ash is magical, but because our Norse forefathers once believed it held the world together, rooted in the underworld and touching heaven. . . . Its buds, as Lord Tennyson observed, are black' (*Possession* 95). The reference to Tennyson initiates a familiar intertextual process whereby a real-life figure and a fictitious one are mutually juxtaposed. The former appears to confirm the reality of the latter, and thereby creates a false but temporary effect of verisimilitude.

The possibilities surrounding Christabel's name are exciting, and they are several. Ash himself, in the manner of a poet steeped in literary tradition, draws attention to the parallel with 'Coleridge's heroine of his unfinished poem' (*Possession* 175)[2]. For her part, Christabel too alludes to a meeting she had had, as a very young girl, with Coleridge. In one of her letters to Ash she writes, ' "I too have seen S.T.C. I was but an infant – his pudgy hand rested on my golden curls – his Voice remarked on their flaxen paleness – he said. . . . It is a beautiful name and will I trust not be a name of ill omen' " (*Possession* 178–9). Once again the reader encounters a case of the real verifying the fictitious and a juxtaposition of two mutually exclusive categories, of the real and the imaginary.

Following the thread of this interplay between the real and the illusive, it is possible to see a real-life model for Christabel in Christina Rossetti. The similarity of Christian names is an obvious place to begin. This extends beyond the superficial one of nomenclature to the type of poetry that Christina wrote. Like Christabel, Christina too was a minor poetess of the Victorian period. Christina also had a contemporary who was like her in many ways, including spinsterhood, in Emily Dickinson, the American poetess. It has been remarked of Christina that 'by her simplicity and by the circumstances of her life she bears a resemblance to her American contemporary Emily Dickinson' (Klingopulos 88). Christabel's poetry may thus be said to exhibit the qualities of Dickinson's at second remove. One such quality is the generous use of hyphens and capital letters in her poems, a definite 'influence' of Dickinson's poetry. Take the following excerpt from one of Christabel's poems:

> Our Lady – bearing – Pain
> She bore what the Cross bears
> She bears and bears again –
> As the Stone – bears – its scars

The Hammer broke her out
Of rough Rock's ancient – Sleep –
And chiselled her about
With stars that weep – that weep – (*Possession* 381)

Byatt achieves a further remarkable take-off on Dickinson in a Christabel-authored poem called 'I like things clean about me'. It brings to memory one of Dickinson's best-known poems, 'Because I could not stop for Death' (Dickinson 350). Christabel's poem too speaks of death as a 'Guest' who is awaited, and both poems describe their visitor in more or less the same words:

The house is ready spotless
Waiting for the Guest
Who will see our white linen
At its very best
Who will take it and fold it
And lay us to rest. (*Possession* 37)

If the route taken by this association (of Christabel to Christina via Dickinson) seems tortuous, it must be remembered that it is the way of intertextuality to deny a naïve and simplistic relationship. In any case, Christina's writing too has its share in creating and shaping Christabel's. Klingopulos says with perfect truth, 'Christina achieved her most popular success in imitations of ballads with a suggestion of allegory, such as "Goblin Market" and "The Prince's Progress" ' (Klingopulos 88). Christabel's forte too lies in these genres.

Indeed, 'Goblin Market' is the text that comes most readily to mind when any of Christabel's writing is encountered in *Possession*. The sense of lurking evil, of succumbing to it and suffering its consequences in a pre-Christian fairy-tale milieu, which is characteristic of 'Goblin Market', is prevalent in Christabel's narratives and poetry[3]. Her *Melusina* is a case in point. No less typical is 'The Glass Coffin', which is the first sustained textual introduction of Christabel to the reader of *Possession*. This is a prose narrative set in the fairy-tale mode, spanning nearly ten pages (*Possession* 58–67)[4].

The foregoing example illustrates various devices of intertextuality, in concurrent operation as it were:

a) A name in the text under discussion which intelligibly resembles a previous name, either from life or another text, and with which an association is then built up.
b) Textual evidences to buttress this resemblance, which could otherwise be dismissed as a coincidence; the resemblance here being the two names with identical first syllables /Krist/.

c) The juxtaposition of 'Christabel' and 'Christina', and their respective ontological categories, of illusion (fiction) and reality (real life). Christabel in fact owes her intertextual identity to a name in Coleridge's poem as well as two historical nineteenth-century poetesses. Thus the categories of illusion and reality both invest the name 'Christabel' with intertextual echoes.

d) Reinforcement: Christabel, like her ancestors Christina and Dickinson, is perceived with twentieth-century hindsight as 'modern'[5].

FLW too has its share of intertextual names. Charles Smithson owes his Christian name to a major Victorian novelist ('Dickens') and a leading Victorian scientist ('Darwin'), while his servant, Sam, brings to mind Sam Weller from Dickens's *The Pickwick Papers*. The case is slightly different with *Tess* and *Heathcliff*, where names are predetermined because of the allegiance to one definite source-text.

As intertextual devices, names function as pointers to the interdependence of texts. Even Christabel's dog is named from Shakespeare's *King Lear*: 'The Little dogs and all – Tray, Blanche and Sweetheart, see they bark at me' (*King Lear* 3.6.65–66, quoted in *Possession* 352).

Finally there is Maud, the heroine of the twentieth-century story of *Possession*. Maud Bailey takes her name from Tennyson's poem of the same title. This is a fact that her admirers, all inhabiting the world of academia, compulsively acknowledge, by using the poet's words to describe her as 'icily regular, splendidly null' (*Possession* 316, 506). Maud's name is an illustration of the extent to which textual identity can stretch itself. The reader accepts Maud as 'real' only in a provisional sense, for the purposes of *Possession*. She is no more real than Tennyson's 'Maud' – or in other words, she is as fictitious a character as Tennyson's, the only difference being that they belong to two different fictional texts. Yet the reader of *Possession* is required to forget selectively that the 'Maud' he encounters is (also) fictitious. Against the normal trend of a textual figure owing her name and identity to a real-life one, the 'real' Maud he encounters in this novel is described in terms of a fictitious character in Tennyson's poem.

The Quotation

Arguably the most obvious and direct of intertextual devices, quotations are not always acknowledged as external textual property. Sometimes, even within inverted commas, a quotation can remain incognito for an uninitiated reader, taking us back to the question of optimal relevance and intertextuality. One such teaser from *Possession* is 'icily regular, splendidly null', which is quoted with reference to Maud Bailey. There is no indication anywhere in the novel that this poetic turn of phrase is from Tennyson's poem, even though it is quoted more than once in *Possession* (316, 506).

Unobtrusively present and little-known quotations like this can jeopardise intertextuality, since they do not announce the source from where they are imported. It takes a pertinacious reader to discover their relevance, as otherwise they are lost in the text and can become invisible. This can thwart the purposes of intertextuality, which depends precisely on the identification of the quotation.

For the purposes of intertextuality, a quotation that does not advertise its presence may as well not exist. An intertextual event can occur only when an'other' text is *perceived* as occupying a space within a given text. In an intertextually-driven hierarchy of quotations, a quote without inverted commas is lowest in the ladder. Thereafter comes the quotation that preserves the punctuation marks around it, thereby declaring its loyalty to its predecessor-text. The top-rung is occupied by a quotation that not only retains its markers, but also acknowledges its author.

Intertextuality has much to do with the third kind of quotation. This type is imported completely into the new text, and its motive in being present becomes a significant matter for discussion. When it arrives thus into the new text, it brings along with it a baggage of meanings whose relevance to the later text needs to be deciphered by the reader. With other, less direct quotations, mere identification can be an issue, but not with this. Victorianism becomes a lively event to observe when the author subjects a Victorian quotation to intertextual transformation.

Tennant provides a brilliant example in her quotations describing Tess's mouth (Tennant 57). She supplies excerpts within inverted commas from *Tess of the d'Urbervilles* in which Hardy portrays the enchanting mouth of Tess Durbeyfield from various angles (8, 9, 49, 89, 148, 166). But Tennant's motive is patently in polar opposition to Hardy's. Hardy's aim in this description is to evoke the vision of a seductive, yet innocent young girl: indeed, part of her entrancing charm is her sexual ignorance. In Tennant's narrative, these quotations become feminist weapons to be used against Hardy, lending themselves to subtle but sure manipulation towards exposing Hardy's personal voyeurism.

The Letter

The letter is an informal text of considerable distinction due to its literary lineage. The first English novel appeared in epistolary form with Richardson, and subsequently too, letters have played an integral role in the structure of the novel. Letters continued to play a pivotal role in directing narrative courses through the eighteenth and nineteenth countries. *Pride and Prejudice* and *Tess of the d'Urbervilles* are just two examples of novels whose plots would flounder, if the letters they contain were taken out.

As a form, the letter is characterised by an informality that is absent in other genres such as the dramatic monologue or the sonnet. This is specially the case with the personal letter. The personal letter holds a sense of trust and confidence, which it conveys to the reader. When confronted with a letter containing some information, the reader tends naturally to credit it with authenticity/genuineness of emotion, more than he would, for instance, give an inserted quotation or, to take an extreme case, a fairy tale.

Like the journal, the epistle is a text characterised by privacy and intimacy. It cannot be as private as the journal, since the journal is meant to be read by nobody but its writer. In fact, 'reading' is an incidental part of the journal-text, as its essential purpose is expression through writing. In the case of the letter however, communication assumes primary significance. While a letter, especially a personal one, is no less a means of emotional outlet than a journal, it is also meant to be read by its addressee.

The letter becomes a formidable intertextual tool in at least two Victorianist novels. One of these is *Heathcliff*. Heathcliff's letter to Cathy appropriates a substantial portion of Haire-Sargeant's narrative, and helps the novel admirably in responding to its parent text, Emily Brontë's *Wuthering Heights*. Essentially, Heathcliff's letter purports to tackle two issues that *Wuthering Heights* leaves open to its reader's conjecture. These two unanswered questions are: a) What are Heathcliff's origins? b) Where did he make his fortune?

As *Wuthering Heights* makes clear, Cathy is the only person in the world to whom Heathcliff would bare his soul without reserve. Lin Haire-Sergeant follows this logic set by the earlier novel, and creates a situation in her *Heathcliff* where Heathcliff answers both these questions in a letter to Cathy. But Ellen Dean intercepts this letter, and its contents become common knowledge – to Lockwood and Charlotte Brontë.

In the unlikely if not impossible companionship of Lockwood (a fictional character) and Charlotte Brontë (a real figure and also an author) we have once again a typically intertextual event, where two mutually exclusive categories are brought together to produce a self-reflexive effect. Here it is the letter which makes this possible, for, in fact, *Heathcliff* begins with Lockwood showing the letter to Charlotte Brontë.

As a testimony to the truth about Heathcliff, the letter serves a two-fold purpose. On the mimetic level of the narrative, it functions as an indispensable text that possesses exclusive information. Heathcliff's letter alone can bridge the gap in knowledge left open by the *ur*-text, *Wuthering Heights.* This is verified by default, as it were, when Ellen burns a portion of the letter, and the information lost forever is bitterly rued by Lockwood. However, before Ellen can completely destroy the letter Cathy enters the room and saves the remaining part; thus we have an intriguing situation where a fictional figure, namely, Cathy, is entrusted with the 'responsibility' of salvaging some of the valuable information the text can provide. Secondly, by virtue of its formal properties and attributes – especially sincerity – the letter as a text holds considerable narrative authority. Implicit in the assumption behind making Heathcliff write a letter, is Haire-Sergeant's understanding that in a letter, Heathcliff will not lie.

A second Victorianist novel wherein the letter becomes an intertextual apparatus is *Possession*. The entire love affair of Christabel and Ash is revealed to the reader in the most 'suitable' text, which is the epistle. The letters they write each other are appropriately intimate, expressing their innermost, unmediated feelings, and form all of chapter ten of *Possession*, entitled 'The Correspondence'. Exclusively epistolary in formal design, this chapter painstakingly registers the acquaintance of Ash and Christabel, growing into friendship and culminating in love. Let us look at them in more detail.

Beginning an early letter decorously with 'Dear Miss LaMotte' (*Possession* 157), Ash gradually changes the form of greeting to 'My dear Friend' (181), until emboldened to venture 'My dear' (199). Christabel initially writes 'Dear Mr Ash' (178), but eventually responds with equal ardour in 'Dearest Sir' (199). A short-lived resistance on her part to Ash's overtures is prompted by her friend Blanche's interception of one of his letters, as well as the manuscript copy of his poem 'Swammerdam'. But it is almost immediately overcome: 'I have an Apology to make that I wish to make in Person. Here is your Olive-branch. Will you receive it?' (*Possession* 190). Signing this letter as 'Your true friend' (190), Christabel sets a seal on this romance. The narrator, it must be observed, keeps scrupulously out of this intimate text.

These letters show how the same person can write like two different people, depending on whether he is writing a poem or a letter. Ash, the poet, has marvellous control over his craft, showing himself adept at handling even a challenging text like the dramatic monologue with commendable aplomb. However, his letters render him terribly vulnerable and emotional. The highly polished verse of the poet gives way to all the emotion of an impulsive letter-writer in chapter ten of *Possession*.

Take the following example. When Christabel is overcome temporarily by Blanche's insinuations, and her own confused mental state, she makes a suggestion to Ash that they cease all correspondence. Ash responds with agitation: 'I will confess, I was at first not only shocked, but angry, that you should write *so*' (*Possession* 185) and later on emphatically adds, 'No—my dear Miss LaMotte—I do not (on the evidence you have offered) think it would be better if we were to cease to correspond. It would not be better for me—' (*Possession* 185). Christabel is equally at the mercy of her emotion-tossed mind. In a reply to Ash, she mentions that it is 'not the first time this letter has been embarked on: I know neither how to start nor how to proceed' (*Possession* 189).

This very letter also resorts to a remarkable gesture that calls attention to its textuality. Having written the beginning of a sentence, Christabel decides to strike it out. Although she crosses the words with her pen, the words themselves remain in the text: ~~'But to stoop to Theft'~~ (*Possession* 189).

This raises a new aspect of textuality and writing that is closely related to the notion of a palimpsest, namely erasure. The integrity of a letter is not damaged in displaying evidence of revision or re-evaluation, particularly in the case of a novel like *Possession* that admits of self-reflexivity. Editing is an inevitable stage in any writing process, and few (if any) literary works can boast the absence of manuscript revision[6]. Yet, convention and perhaps also convenience demand that this stage be hidden from the final version of the text. So in all final versions, the text as it eventually comes to stay has, for practical purposes, forgotten its older, hesitant incarnations. This convention is flouted at this juncture by this particular letter. By retaining the impulsive words on the page, as well as the tell-tale strikethrough sign that as an afterthought they were obliterated, it may be ventured that Byatt shares her own writing experience with the reader.

If this is so, then no textual device can help her so well as the letter (except perhaps the journal). Byatt can dare such an interpolation within the confines of the letter-text knowing that letters possess an aura of informality, even within the most literary of texts, which will permit the transgression of an unwritten rule. The letter is a valuable intertextual device at this juncture, showing up, among other things, a rare ability to unmask a layer of textuality. The only other textual device that shares this privilege is the journal.

Christabel's palimpsestic move deserves attention in the context of intertextuality. Erasure is complementary to writing, particularly to creative writing, which consists for the most part of over-writing. The palimpsest is an apt symbol of all intertextual proceedings since it suggests the coexistence and inter-relatedness of more than one text. From an intertextual point of view, the prior text has perforce to suffer a degree of erasure in the process of being re-inscribed, and the resulting design is that of a palimpsest.

Erasure and revision are concepts that are introduced sufficiently early into the narrative of *Possession*, in the preliminary drafts of Ash's letter that incite Roland's curiosity. Right at the beginning of the novel, he comes to the London library as usual, engaged in his work on Randolph Henry Ash. Suddenly while reading Ash's poem 'Proserpina', Roland chances upon two letters folded delicately within the poem. Both are in Ash's writing, though unsigned, and address a nameless 'Dear Madam'. The plot of *Possession* is thereafter devoted to an unfolding of the identity of the mysterious lady, and her relationship with Ash. The very incompleteness of the letter becomes (in intertextual accordance) a principal motivating force for Roland and other characters to embark on the quest for the truth.

What Roland comes across in the London library are, therefore, not two letters, but two versions or earlier drafts of the letter that Ash was eventually to send to Christabel. Neither of these two sample letters is sent to Christabel, because they have been superseded by a more suitable draft that Ash eventually despatches. Yet the specimen letters are retained within the novel not only to trigger the plot, but also to stress the importance of erasure and revision in writing. As prefatory exercises in striking a friendship with Christabel, these letters show that every text has a redundant part to it(*Possession* 5–6).

The most rewarding aspect of the letters to the reader of *Possession* is their generous store of literary allusions, which constitute the most obvious kind of intertextuality. Christabel does not want to stop corresponding with Ash, but being a Victorian woman, she feels socially constrained to halt before the friendship becomes an emotional threat. She therefore writes to Ash, 'Think of me if you will as the Lady of Shalott – with a Narrower Wisdom – who chooses not the Gulp of outside Air and the chilly river-journey deathwards – but who chooses to watch diligently the bright colours of her Web' (*Possession* 187). A literary reference like this is a form of intensified intertextuality: a reference (to Tennyson's poem) within a sub-genre (letter) within a novel (*Possession*).

Allusions abound in 'The Correspondence' to the Bible, classical mythology, the plays of Shakespeare, the poetry of George Herbert, and the writing of such 'contemporaries' as John Stuart Mill and Ruskin. For brief periods, other texts bring their ambience into the elastic easy-going letter. When Christabel writes to Ash about their meeting, she describes the weather in terms that are truer to poetry than a letter, and resonate to pathetic fallacy. The Thames, writes Christabel, has been advancing rapidly, 'climbing. . . with watery ferocity – and laughing and slapping its way across the cobbled pavements on the bank – invading people's gardens, paying no attention to wicket-gates or wooden fence – but creeping sinuously – and bubbling up – brown and strong – bringing with it a trail of *such things*. . .' (*Possession* 190). The verbs accurately describe the turmoil in Christabel's heart and mind as she prepares, after much correspondence, to meet Ash in person for the first time.

The letters also function as enveloping texts or frame-texts, thereby fulfilling another intertextual requirement of showing two texts existing side by side, or one within another, for some of them contain poems. One missing letter is believed to contain 'Swammerdam', which is lost to the reader who encounters only a finished version of the poem later (*Possession* 202–9).

Towards the beginning of their epistolary exchanges, Christabel encloses two poems, 'Metamorphosis' and 'Psyche' (*Possession* 161–62). As the chapter moves to its end, Christabel writes another poem called 'The Grassy Knoll' dictated by her Muse (*Possession* 201). In an intertextual work, the site of references is of as great significance as the references themselves. 'The grassy knoll' which is full of sexual imagery and connotation is placed at the end of the Ash–Christabel letters as a means of anticipating the physical consummation of their affair. The affair itself is reported by the omniscient Victorian authorial voice, and this shift from one textual mode to another is a pointer to the limitations of the letter.

In their capacity as poets, Ash and Christabel grant their letters the status of a resource-text which are of value to research students and scholars like Roland and Maud. Distanced from these poets by an intervening century, the young scholars would have had to depend on second-hand, derived interpretations of Ash's or Christabel's poetry. This is where their letters clarify the picture, and throw light upon the motives as well as the influences on their writing. When Ash's letter endeavours to explain the circumstances under which his poem *Ragnarök* was written, the reader comes to realise that his poetry was misunderstood even by contemporary 'educated' peers like Christabel. His explanation becomes an intertextual phenomenon as the poem, in order to be correctly understood, depends upon the letter that functions like a gloss.

Ash writes with concern, '*Ragnarök* was written in all honesty in the days when I did not myself question Biblical certainties' (*Possession* 163). But certain readers saw things otherwise: 'I was at the time startled and surprised that my Poem should have been construed as any kind of infidelity – for I meant it rather as a reassertion of the Universal Truth of the living presence of Allfather (under whatever Name) and of the hope of Resurrection from whatever whelming disaster in whatever form' (*Possession* 163). For later students of Ash's writings, this pronouncement would come as a boon in settling arguments and debates on the intention of *Ragnarök*.

The letters are all undated. At first glance this is disconcerting, but upon reflection, this is seen to endow them with the universality especially useful in literary discussions on the nature of writing. For example, discussing *Ragnarök* and its impact Ash writes: 'This is a two-handed engine, a slicing weapon that cuts both ways, this of figuration – to say that the Truth of the Tale is in the meaning, that the Tale but symbolises an eternal verity, is one step on the road to the parity of all tales. . .' (*Possession* 163).

There are other letters in *Possession* besides those of Ash and Christabel to each other. The 'public' letter of Ash to Mrs Cropper is one of these (*Possession* 103–5). There are also letters that merely provide information, like that of Ariane Le Minier (379–80). Ash's letters to his wife while he is away are in the style of travelogues (460–61). The Ash–Christabel letters are unique in carrying the weight of both romantic and literary passion. In their hands the letter emerges as a protean text, subject to the needs of the situation that creates it.

The Journal

Another text that *Possession* dialogues with is comparable to the letter in its informal nature, and this is the journal. There is however one crucial difference. The letter is intrinsically dialogic in character, while the journal is monologic and self-centred.

Keeping a diary became habitual in the seventeenth-century, and women kept some of the best diaries in the eighteenth and the nineteenth centuries. Particularly in the Victorian period, the diary became a recognised text of the female domain. Male writers regarded it as a 'safe' text, for it permitted self-expression for the female in a highly circumscribed manner. The journal nevertheless functioned as a therapeutic text for women writers, offering itself as a means of emotional outlet. Its historical importance rests in postmodern fashion on its marginal position in a patriarchal community, which grudgingly allows women to write away from the male bastion of more public forms such as poetry or the novel.

Possession exploits the textual and intertextual reaches of the journal exhaustively. There are two prominent diaries embedded in its narrative, those of Ellen Ash and Sabine. Ellen's journal is a complementary text to Ash's writings. At the same time, in another of its intertextual guises, it lends itself as a weapon to be used by feminist readers. In one of her journal entries, Ellen records a dream where she plays chess with Herbert Baulk. He decrees that her Queen can move only one square, like his King. This is contrary to the rules of the game, where the Queen has a sweeping freedom of movement unlike the King, and Baulk's order, unjust and patriarchal, shows how deeply Ellen has internalised the unfair nature of the society she belongs to (*Possession* 228).

Byatt invests this journal with a very Victorianist identity by showing how, even in a journal, the Victorian psyche can never shed all its inhibitions and be self-damagingly frank. Ellen is unable to bring herself to write two secrets, her own inadequacy in having a sexual relationship with her husband, and her knowledge of the adulterous affair of Ash and Christabel. For a full divulging of facts, the reader has to wait till the omniscient Victorian author takes the narrative thread onwards[7].

As previously stated, the 'texture' of the journal has several threads in common with the letter despite obvious differences. Byatt reinforces this with erasure, the device that earlier figured in the elucidation of Ash and Christabel's letters. In her journal, Ellen Ash too strikes the beginning of a sentence: '~~Despite all~~ We have been so happy in our life together. . .' (*Possession* 229). The visible erasure, an oxymoron *par excellence*, becomes a powerful textual device working against the intentions of its author. Ellen is unable to admit her sexual frigidity to a text, but the exigencies of the journal do exercise a degree of power over her that she cannot uniformly resist.

'Despite all' is an inadvertent slip, the words escaping her before she can stop herself. This circumstance suffices to establish a multifaceted relationship between Ellen and the journal. On one level the journal is her confidante, but on another it is an adversary that puts her on her guard. In this struggle, the journal secures a near-triumph when Ellen writes words that need to be removed. Eventually however her personality overcomes the journal's textual force. If *Possession* has attempted to employ the journal as an intertextual device to 'tell all', it is doomed to fail; as in the case of the letters, boundaries operate in obedience to the Victorian milieu.

There is one other erasure in Ellen's journal: ~~'I should have'~~ (*Possession* 231). This registers the battle between conscience and duty in Ellen's mind, as she wonders whether she should have shown greater kindness to Bertha, her unwed, pregnant maid. Here the journal brings the immediacy of Victorian society and its morality before the reader. Byatt deliberately introduces these erasures into Ellen's journal, although she knows that they could have been concealed. Elsewhere within the journal the omniscient author makes an entry: '[Passage crossed out illegibly]' (*Possession* 231). But Ellen's passages are not 'crossed out illegibly'.

Just as Ellen refuses to trust her journal with the secret of her sexual apathy, she also withholds the truth about Ash and Christabel from it. In an entry made in June, she writes about the visits presumably of Blanche Glover, Christabel's friend. Blanche who is fiercely possessive about Christabel has resorted to various tactics, including physical force, to break the romance between Christabel and Ash. There are overtones of lesbianism in the friendship of Blanche and Christabel, underscored in her visit, which is a bid to secure Christabel for herself by informing Ellen about her husband's infidelity. Of this Ellen writes baldly: 'My importunate visitor came and we talked some time. That matter is now I hope quite at an end and wholly cleared up' (*Possession* 231). Ellen's real emotions do occasionally 'slip' out onto the text, but the general tone of her journal is one of a public record, consisting of commonplace items like domestic worries or intelligent musings on writers. The public voice shapes the journal into a less impulsive and more 'proper' text[8].

The diary maintained by Sabine, on the other hand, is a chameleon-text that is steeped in romance and feminism. The period that Christabel spends with Sabine serves as an unofficial literary apprenticeship for the latter, therefore some very interesting ideas on the nature of writing and literature are located in Sabine's journal. They are irregular entries and do not seem structured; this is in keeping with the fluidity of the journal-form. For instance one entry begins: 'The pleasures of writing are various. The language of reflection has its own pleasure and the language of narration quite a different one' (*Possession* 344). After this promising preamble, the rest of the entry digresses into a description of Christabel.

Byatt's judicious adaptation of the journal as an intertextual device leads her into areas of literary criticism and theory. The most self-conscious portion of Sabine's diary is in the entry entitled 'Toussaint', where she examines the idea of narrative truth. Her father tells the story of Merlin and Vivien every winter. But, as Sabine discovers, though 'always the same tale,' it is never 'twice the same telling' (*Possession* 353). Within the framework of this narrative, Sabine's father imaginatively varies the pattern. Sometimes Vivien is a faithful lover of Merlin, at other times she is a manipulating schemer. Sabine's tribute to her father's creative powers is pertinently offered in the metaphor of a threshold:

> My father was lavish with imagined primroses and bluebells; he made birds sing in dark hollies and yews, so that I remembered my childhood life which was lived *in* tales, so that I saw flowers and fountains and hidden paths and figures of power and despised – no, diminished in my mind, the life of real things, the house, the orchard, Gode.
>
> (*Possession* 354)

As mentioned earlier, the threshold is a metaphor for all intertextual proceedings, as it draws attention to boundaries, margins and openings.

The same entry carries an emphatic assertion from Sabine about the importance of segregating meaning from story, and invites the reader to approach *Possession* in the same anti-mimetic way; to consider the interplay between the multiple texts within a novel, and note their mutual assistance in building narrative blocks. Truth inheres in no one text entirely, and meaning cannot reach an ultimate signified. The craving for '*explanations*' must not be indulged, for they diminish (*Possession* 355). Such a desire itself is reductionist in its approach.

Plurality of texts is an intertextual concept that implies a fragmented structure, since one voice will have to break off where another begins. Byatt literally amuses herself and the reader with the contradictory effects of this proceeding. In one instance, the break is used to intensify the illusion of reality within the text, the text in point being the letter. Christabel's poem, 'The Grassy Knoll', is a twice-embedded text, a poem *within* a letter *within* a novel. Byatt's experimentation takes the text at this juncture to a heightened (if temporary) effect of 'reality', since the poem authenticates the letter-writer and grounds her with a firm identity as a poet. The opposite impact is caused in Sabine's journal where the interruption disrupts the illusion. The diary seems to regress into other texts infinitely, as inside the novel there is a story by Gode about a sailor who tells stories. Then, abruptly, there is a 'Note by Ariane Le Minier' to say that 'Here there are some pages missing, and what is written becomes perfunctory and repetitive' (*Possession* 368). The gap in the journal can work self-reflexively to show that just as Maud and Roland are only reading a journal, albeit a very absorbing one, we too are reading a 'clever' novel.

The Biography and the Autobiography

Two inter-related textual devices that closely follow the letter and the journal, with respect to personal intimacy, are the biography and the autobiography. Byatt ably foregrounds their intertextual potential in *Possession*. Mortimer Cropper's biography of Ash is a fitting instance to examine this statement. Entitled *The Great Ventriloquist,* it seems to incarnate the principle of ventriloquism in the genre it chooses, since the conventions of the biography require that one voice speak with authority for (and over) another (voice), for which ventriloquism is a fitting metaphor.

Among the several textual excerpts from *The Great Ventriloquist* in *Possession* is an apparently authoritative passage on Ash's honeymoon to the Sorgue. Cropper draws a series of literary parallels between the fountain in Sorgue and 'Coleridge's sacred river', 'the Fountain of the Muses' and Petrarch's love for Laura (*Possession* 108–9). So far it is fine. But when Cropper begins to interpret the personal life of Ash and Ellen, he is clearly out of his depth. 'Did Ellen Best's prim delicacy', writes Cropper, 'a little past its flowering, hide an unexpected ardour of response? Perhaps it did' (*Possession* 110). It did nothing of the kind: as the reader discovers, Ellen could never have a sexual relationship.

The reader has to cover almost three hundred and fifty pages of the novel to appreciate the ironic thrust of Cropper's (mis)conjecture, when the omniscient narrator records a succession of abortive attempts by Ellen and Ash at sexual consummation. The truth of the honeymoon, over which Cropper waxes eloquent, is something altogether unusual. '*A respite*, generously agreed, glasses of golden wine, a few days of Edenic picnics, a laughing woman perched on a rock in pale blue poplin skirts, a handsome man in his whiskers, lifting her, quoting Petrarch' (*Possession* 459, emphasis mine). The operative phrase is 'A respite'; it is a strange honeymoon indeed, where the couple have mutually agreed to refrain from making love.

Byatt uses biography in order to mock the absurd pretensions of Mortimer Cropper, and also to show that as a text imparting information it is incomplete, and requires the omniscient narrative to set the record right for the mystified reader. Cropper quotes from Ellen's letter home, 'that her husband was "exquisitely considerate in all things" '. This, he says, 'we can read how we choose' (*Possession* 110). There is little doubt over how Cropper chooses to read it. His query, 'Had they come from a night of bliss?' (*Possession* 110), is purely rhetorical; he believes that in fact they have come from a night of bliss. The real facts of the case remain a secret to the characters in the novel and are shared only with the reader. In a reversal of generic expectations, Byatt privileges her novel over biography in possessing the 'right' information. This is a reversal, because biography is the genre normally associated with factual truth. Here, however, fiction is granted precedence over fact in possessing the truth.

As is the case with the three textual devices discussed so far, the letter, the journal and the biography, the autobiography too is 'already' intertextual by being enclosed and framed within the main narrative of *Possession*. *The Shadowy Portal* is the autobiography of Mrs Lees, a spiritualist and a medium who conducts séances. That section of it, which is afforded to the reader, pertains to a particular séance sitting that she conducted, which was deliberately disrupted by Ash.

The title of her autobiography has a symbolic relevance to the textual design of *Possession*, and assists as a paradigm for reading the entire novel. Intertextuality depends on the identification of more than one text (at least) within a single frame. For this to happen, margins, i.e. 'thresholds' and 'portals' are of vital significance as markers in terminating one text and initiating the next.

Byatt deploys the concept of a threshold or a portal with unfailing zest right through the novel. It is especially prominent in the fairy tale written by Christabel. 'The Shadowy Portal' is in any case an appropriate title for a text concerned with the twilight zone, which spirits are traditionally believed to inhabit. This idea is internally validated by the text when Lees asks, 'Do not ghosts appear at twilight, and the Celtic races meet the messengers of the dead in what they call the Black Month?' (*Possession* 394).

The metaphoric extent of Lees's vocation is brought to light in Ash's response to the underlying beliefs of conducting a séance. Lees declares, 'I have no power to summon spirits. I am their instrument; they speak through me, or not, as they please, not as I please'. And Ash replies, 'They speak to me too, through the medium of language' (*Possession* 395). The pun on 'medium' has already been described in the chapter, 'The Dramatic Monologue'. That creative writing is enabled by a source of energy beyond human reach is not a new idea in literary history.

Owing to its location in *Possession*, Lees's autobiographical account of her séance as disturbed, even desecrated by Ash, assumes the nature of an intertextual dialogue. A few pages before presenting her account, *Possession* features Ash's letter to Ruskin about the same episode, which dismisses the whole spiritualist proceeding as 'trickery' (*Possession* 391). Ash says, 'I am convinced as I may be that we are all being practised upon – I will not say by a simple fraud – but by someone who lives by such practising' (*Possession* 390). This is also the background for reading 'Mummy Possest', for by explaining that Ash was disposed to discredit mediumistic practices, it offers one explanation for an unflattering portrayal of the medium in 'Mummy Possest'. Ash's letter thereby becomes a portal for bringing the dramatic monologue into the narrative.

In fact there is more than one dialogue of an intertextual nature at this juncture. Ash's own letter is located in Cropper's biography, which in turn is located in *Possession*. Ash's letter is followed by the omniscient narrative, and then comes Lees's description, in her autobiography, of Ash's unruly behaviour. Her version of the incident is naturally diametrically opposed to Ash's. She prefaces the 'Gaza Exploit', as it came to be termed, with supposedly 'scientific' remarks on the disruptive impact of scepticism on a séance. Ash antagonises her by setting himself up as a belligerent disbeliever, issuing moreover the counter-claim that spirits can communicate with him too. The reader is prevented from abstracting an unambiguous verdict on the matter by Byatt's introduction of another text. In the middle of her séance, Lees falls into a trance, and the onus of reporting subsequent events is on Miss Judge, whose voice takes charge of the hitherto autobiographical account (*Possession* 396–97). Olivia Judge is supposedly a comparatively neutral party, and her account is factual. Her intrusion at this juncture lends the rest of the account, at least, an impression of truth, due to authorial displacement. The intertextual pattern is also intensified, with one more example of a 'narrative-within-narrative-within-narrative' (Judge's account within Lees's autobiography which is in *Possession*). Intertextuality comes to be foregrounded by the proliferation of margins, breaks and beginnings.

The Footnote

The footnote becomes a flexible and occasionally unrecognisable text in the hands of Fowles in *FLW*. In chapter twenty-six, he investigates the etymological source of the word 'blackmail', leaving the reader under no illusion that this is irrelevant to the story. The parenthesis in the first sentence states this boldly: '*Mal* (if I may add to your stock of useless knowledge) is an Old English borrowing from Old Norwegian. . .' (*FLW* 182–83), and the rest of the paragraph traces the history of this word.

In terms of content, this paragraph indubitably belongs to the textual category of the footnote. And since *FLW* uses footnotes quite lavishly for a novel, it is surprising that Fowles should stint at adding one more. By retaining a virtual footnote in the main body of the narrative, Fowles does not imply that the note and the main text are interchangeable. Despite his mystification technique, the footnote is still recognised as a footnote by a perceptive reader, whose attention is attracted to Fowles's unorthodox treatment of this intertextual device. By not using this text where he would most naturally be expected to use it, Fowles makes the footnote conspicuous by its absence; and a missing footnote at the bottom of this page is all the more remarkable in the face of its presence in the middle of the page.

Versatility is a fundamental trait of this intertextual tool as it comes to be used by Fowles. His self-proclaimed mission in writing *FLW* is to produce a Victorian novel that the Victorians failed to write. One implication of this assertion is that hindsight has endowed him with more knowledge about the Victorians than any of their contemporaries. To encode this knowledge, no text can be better employed than the footnote. Although characterised by economy, its major purpose is to provide additional information. By enabling his novel to dialogue with the Victorian period, it becomes a handy intertextual tool for Fowles.

This apart, its spatial position offers a leeway for intertextuality to operate, because its way of supplying information is by dissociation from the body of the main text. The footnote encourages the reader to digress, if only for a short while, from the narrative. An engrossed reader may make an inward protest at being demanded to swerve from the novel. But such is the conventionally acknowledged importance of the footnote that he will invariably resign himself to reading it. A reader unwise enough to disregard a footnote does so at his own expense, knowing that he has lost something of value despite loyally adhering to the main body of the text. Thus the power of the footnote is not negligible even though it plays a supplementary textual role. At the same time, since a beguiled reader may well be tempted to go on with the main text, the footnote has to struggle in order to captivate the reader.

The relationship between the text and the footnote is thus ambivalent. It is symbiotic to a certain extent, as both need each other; nevertheless the text and the footnote are also inimical to each other because both simultaneously vie for attention. The footnote has a natural place in a scholarly journal such as the one simulated by Byatt in *Possession* (443-46). But in a novel its role would normally be detrimental to narrative interest. One of the primary conditions for reading a novel is a 'willing suspension of disbelief'. The success of a conventional novel depends on the extent and duration to which the reader can credit the illusory as real. This is especially the case with the traditional Victorian novel. On the other hand, a metafictional novel actively discourages a suspension of disbelief on the reader's part. *FLW* is a Victorianist rather than a Victorian novel, and it is characterised by self-reflexivity. It 'flamboyantly plays on the specious temporal distance between the world it creates and the world in which the apparatus of invention is constructed' (Conradi in '*The French Lieutenant's Woman*: novel, screenplay, film' 43).

Within the first fifty pages of *FLW*, there are as many as three footnotes. The first footnote is an elaborate description of the protagonist Charles as 'a healthy agnostic' (*FLW* 18). The footnote meticulously elucidates: 'Though he would not have termed himself so, for the very simple reason that the word was not coined (by Huxley) until 1870; by which time it had become much needed' (*FLW* 18). This footnote performs its mandatory function of giving supplementary information that need not, strictly speaking, be incorporated within the text. But sometimes, by a strange paradox, what is integral to the meaning of the main text may be placed with greater effect as a footnote. This is one of those paradoxical instances. The main text of *FLW*, which is the narrative, strives insistently to remind the reader that he is only reading a novel and the footnote assists as a reminder by being an intrusive text. The example just provided reinforces metafiction by highlighting an anachronism: that of referring to Charles as an 'agnostic' before the word came into being. The footnote reiterates that Charles could not have called himself an 'agnostic' because he predates the coinage of the word.

The second footnote in *FLW* is a Victorianist comment on the Victorian emphasis of 'duty', even in sexual matters. This footnote is intertextually wider than the previous one, for its reach is not restricted to the narrative. It interacts also with another inherently intertextual device, the epigraph, by directly alluding to it. Chapter five, in which this footnote figures, has two epigraphs, the first being a quotation from Tennyson's *In Memoriam* (*FLW* 27), to which this footnote makes an allusion. This means that the reader has to keep three texts in perspective, all at the same time: the epigraph, the narrative, and the footnote.

A similar intertextual role, though not quite identical, is played by the footnote in chapter thirty-nine, which also interacts directly with the epigraph (*FLW* 259). The text of this epigraph is a letter in a newspaper (yet another textual mode), and the note typically refers readers to the source of this letter, *Human Documents of the Victorian Golden Age* (quoted in *FLW* 259).

Textual juggling becomes more involved and intricate in the third footnote. Once more the question revolves on duty. The sentence marked for elucidation is: 'We meet here, once again, this bone of contention between the centuries: is duty to drive us, or not?' (*FLW* 45–46). In the footnote, the narrator invites a third text to answer the question. This is George Eliot's epigram: 'God is inconceivable, immortality is unbelievable, but duty is peremptory and absolute.'

The footnote to La Ronciere's trial in chapter twenty-eight acts as a concluding comment on the entire, fantastic medical report, detailing a case of female sexual perversion. In a characteristically self-reflexive fashion, this note confuses the worlds of narrative (fiction) and history (reality). Dr Grogan and Charles, who are fictitious characters in the story of *FLW*, are credited with reading the same text as the narrator who has admitted to being a part of the reader's real world. 'I cannot leave the story of La Ronciere – which I have taken from the same 1835 account that Dr Grogan handed Charles' (*FLW* 204). The confusion is perpetrated by the last sentence of the footnote: 'For the both [sic] obscene and absurd ultimate truth of the events of that September night in 1834. . . I must send you to Rene Floriot, *Les Erreurs Judiciaires*, Paris, 1968)' (*FLW* 204).

While there are regular footnotes, which are intertextual simply because of textual displacement[9], the note in chapter forty-eight enlists metafiction to further its intertextual thrust (*FLW* 311–12). It blurs the line between reality and fiction by having a fictional curate allude to a real-life bishop, who 'did not die till two years after the year we are in' (*FLW* 312). Fowles uses this strategy elsewhere in the novel, too, as has already been pointed out in the chapter on the novel.

Footnotes also function as effective intertextual devices in the excerpts from Cropper's biography, *The Great Ventriloquist* (*Possession* 443–46). This passage which discusses another text, the epitaph of Ash, bears an almost parodic resemblance to a scholarly article in an academic journal. Byatt constructs this resemblance through the judicious use of endnotes. Although not footnotes, the endnotes are like them in every respect including documentation. The difference lies in the spatial levels they occupy. Instead of appearing at the end of a page, they appear at the end of an 'article' or chapter.

The citations in these notes enable Byatt to freely include texts ranging from letters (notes 22 and 24) to other journal articles (note 29). Notes 22 to 33 are replete with information on secondary sources that refer back to other texts like newspaper reports, poems, translations, even social texts[10] and internal cross-references. The last ensures that intertextuality repeats itself endlessly, through implication and counter-implication. The notes furthermore classify actual Victorian poets like Swinburne and Tennyson with fictional characters like Ellen Ash: all occupy the same undifferentiated plane of existence. By compelling the real and the illusive to impinge on each other, Byatt underscores the intertextual capabilities of the footnote.

The Epigraph

One of the most common of intertextual devices is the epigraph. Despite its long history its intertextual leanings have not been consciously explored, although they are undoubtedly more pronounced than those of any other text discussed so far. The epigraph originates from an author and text different from the one in which it officiates as an epigraph. In this capacity, it brings an alternate but in some way also connected world-view into the new text. Carrying a textual identity distinct from the text in which it intervenes, the epigraph has the potential to create a textual ripple.

'Unlike a preface or a footnote', comments Deborah Bowen, 'an epigraph almost always originates with a different writer from the text, thus formalising the notion of the 'intertextual event' and consciously admitting a polyphony of voices' (Bowen 69). She refers to epigraphs as 'second-order' textual modes. The epigraph was used prevalently in nineteenth-century fiction but without an acknowledgement of its intertextual potential.

Bowen's own term for an intertextual device is 'paratext' (66–77, 79). Considering the implications of a paratext, Bowen is provoked into quoting Gerard Genette's claim that 'the obligation felt by a reader in relation to a paratextual item is less than the obligation the reader feels toward the text' (Genette, quoted in Bowen 67). Are, then, intertextual devices compulsively assigned a secondary position? This is a valid question regarding the relative significance of intertextual devices, and whether there is an unspoken hierarchy among texts. A categorical answer is impossible, for the opposite point of view carries weight, too: 'a paratext, "the fringe of the printed text", may by its suggestiveness "in reality control the whole reading" ' (quoted in Bowen 67–68).

The epigraph is a Victorian intertext, a specific pointer to the Victorian period[11]. Fowles actually '*reintroduces* the Victorian romantic technique of providing an epigraph not just at the opening of the book but at the opening of each chapter' (Bowen 70, emphasis mine). *Possession* carries two epigraphs at the beginning, as well as individual epigraphs at the commencement of each chapter. In this it superficially resembles *FLW*, but an added complexity in the epigraphic texts of *Possession* is caused by the co-existence of 'real' and 'fictive' epigraphs. While the epigraphs to the novel are from real authors in history, like Hawthorne and Browning, epigraphs to individual chapters are from fictitious writers like Ash and Christabel who have no existence outside the covers of the novel. By incorporating the familiar mechanics of metafiction, Byatt heightens the epigraph's intertextual predisposition.

The first epigraph to the novel is a quotation from Hawthorne's preface to his novel, *The House of the Seven Gables*, describing the generic features of the romance. Since the subtitle of *Possession* is 'A Romance', the first epigraph acts as a link-text between the title and the narrative. By specifically invoking Hawthorne, Byatt accomplishes at least two things. She validates her own use of the romance genre by referring to an outside authority in Hawthorne, thereby showing that texts help texts. At the same time, she defines her own novel as a Victorianist one (if not in so many words) since in Hawthorne's words it attempts 'to connect a bygone time with the very present that is flitting away from us' (Hawthorne 1, quoted in *Possession*). *Possession* is thereby firmly ensconced in generic as well as thematic contexts.

The second epigraph from Browning's poem makes greater inroads into *Possession* than the previous one. 'Mr Sludge, "the Medium"' is intertextually related to 'Mummy Possest', and strengthens the parallel between Ash and Browning. This has been discussed at length in the chapter on the dramatic monologue.

As an intertextual device, the epigraph promotes a type of reverse reading. Its literal meaning is clear at the outset. But its contextual meaning, with respect to the text that follows, becomes clear only after that text is read. This kind of interdependent meaning is true of all intertexts, but particularly so in the case of the epigraph. This is because the epigraph already carries the associations of its original textual location for the educated reader. Its subsequent meaning within the new text may be radically different. The epigraph would then undergo a semantic metamorphosis.

In *FLW*, 'Every emancipation is a restoration of the human world and of human relationships to man himself' from Marx's *Zur Judenfrage* functions as the epigraph to the entire novel. All chapters have epigraphs, some have two. The two sometimes assist each other. At other times, they are mutually opposed. Double epigraphs in 'an ironic paratextual juxtaposition may suggest a paradigm for the novelistic text' (Bowen 75).

Let us first consider the epigraph to chapter thirteen. This chapter is a watershed in *FLW*, where Fowles drastically shatters the narrative illusion by making his hitherto realistic novel metafictional. Nothing in the epigraph prepares the reader for this violence rendered to traditional narrative integrity. The epigraph is from Tennyson's *Maud*: 'For the drift of the Maker is dark, an Isis hid by the veil. . .' (*FLW* 85) and only hindsight teaches the reader not to take the remark literally. Packed with irony, this epigraph belies the narrator's stance in this chapter where he denies his omnipotence as 'Maker', and rather than hide, *reveals* the strings activating his puppets; where he would have the reader 'share my own sense that I do not fully control these creatures of my mind' (*FLW* 87). In this chapter the narrator also believes that 'the novelist is still a god, since he creates. . . what has changed is that we are no longer the gods of the Victorian image, omniscient and decreeing; but in the new theological image, with freedom our first principle, not authority' (*FLW* 86). Although a 'Maker's' existence is conceded, his 'drift' is by no means dark, and the 'veil' is removed (*FLW* 85). The epigraph here is a consummate vehicle of intertextual activity in the way it dialogues with the chapter that it prefaces.

Another example is from chapter two of *FLW* which sports a double epigraph. The first of these belongs to the order of social documentation, providing statistical information about the ratio of Victorian males to females. The excerpt is from E. Royston Pike's *Human Documents of the Victorian Golden Age* and concludes that 'if the accepted destiny of the Victorian girl was to become a wife and mother, it was unlikely that there would be enough men to go round' (*FLW* 10). The second epigraph dramatically differs in form and tone, disrupting the textual mode with which the first epigraph has familiarised the reader. It is a verse lamentation of an instance of unfaithful love. Both epigraphs in their ways thematically point to the turn that the plot of *FLW* will take, and anticipate the romantic triangle of two women and one man, in Ernestina, Sarah and Charles.

Bowen, who has a different interpretation to offer, believes that the terms of both epigraphs are ambiguous. According to her, the second citation suggests a plot in which the man sails away from his lover. This has already 'happened' in *FLW*, in the story that Sarah perpetuates about her French Lieutenant as literally having sailed away from her. When the narrative unfolds, moreover, it is not Charles who leaves Sarah; it is she who leaves him. The implications of the epigraphs are realised in a manner contrary to the expectations that they themselves set up. As Bowen puts it, 'Fowles's skilful evocation of voices muted in the epigraphs springs. . . from an unfolding of their contradictory epistemologies.' (77). Fowles uses these epigraphs to lay a red herring in the reader's path deliberately, and preempt the epigraph from destroying the suspense in the narrative.

In her comprehensive assessment of the epigraphs in *FLW*, Bowen includes the intertext for chapter fifty-five from Lewis Carroll's *Through the Looking-glass*:

> 'Why, about *you*!' Tweedledee exclaimed, clapping his hands triumphantly. 'And if he left off dreaming about you, where do you suppose you'd be?'
>
> 'Where I am now, of course', said Alice.
>
> 'Not you!' Tweedledee retorted contemptuously. 'You'd be nowhere. Why, you're only a sort of thing in his dream!'
>
> 'If that there king was to wake', added Tweedledum, 'you'd go out – bang! – just like a candle!'
>
> 'I shouldn't!' Alice exclaimed indignantly. (*FLW* 346)

The foregoing epigraph presents the polar worlds of dream and reality. Tweedledee and Tweedledum insist to a protesting Alice that she is a figment of the king's dream. This has an analogue within *FLW*, with the omniscient novelist being the 'king', and his characters the creatures of his dream. This epigraph belongs to chapter fifty-five, but Fowles uses it to make a tacit cross-reference to chapter thirteen. One sentence from the latter particularly condones Alice's indignation: 'It is only when our characters and events begin to destroy us that they begin to live' (*FLW* 86).

This epigraph is more complex than it appears. Its content implies that the conditions of Alice's existence are determined by the king. But as readers know, in the larger context of Carroll's *Through The Looking-glass*, Alice is the dreamer. Tweedledum, Tweedledee, the absent king and Alice herself are part of her dream. Contrary to Tweedledum's claim, it is the king and the others who would be 'nowhere' if Alice 'left off dreaming'. Yet the epigraph implies the contrary. As the narrator remarks in chapter thirteen, 'My characters still exist, and in a reality no less, or no more, real than the one I have just broken. Fiction is woven into all. . .' (*FLW* 86–87).

In chapter fifty-five of *FLW* the narrator is shown to occupy a position analogous to Alice's, in that he is 'dreaming' Charles as well as himself in the same dream. The epigraph breaks off before Alice can wake up to be conscious of the border between dream and reality. The narrator's experience is in direct contrast to that of Alice. He permits the awareness of dream to dawn in his consciousness in the course of the chapter, by coming out of his dream: 'And I will keep up the pretence no longer' (*FLW* 348). In its intertextual play this chapter makes fruitful a premise inherent in the epigraph. The epigraph itself cannot make all these points since it is characterised by brevity.

Bowen defines this intertextual event succinctly by articulating Fowles's intention: 'Fiction, he seems to say, is the game we all play' (Bowen 81). Fowles, according to her, is also turning a traditional standpoint on its head. Normally the author is safely perched in reality when he overlooks and directs the course of his fictions. However Fowles 'calls into question not only the fictionality of his characters but also the reality of their analogues' (Bowen 81).

Wessex: Landscape and Intertextuality

In his General Preface to the Wessex edition of 1912, Hardy argues the case for literature by declaring that a small, circumscribed geographical unit is sufficient to represent the world. His own fictionalised landscape, Wessex, is a faithful recasting of the county of Dorset. 'At the dates represented in the various narrations things were like that in Wessex', says Hardy ('General Preface' 479), and claims to have taken no liberty with socio-cultural facts including activities such as mumming in *The Return of the Native*, where Eustacia takes the part of the Turkish Knight (*The Return of the Native* 134–44).

To the question, what aspect of Dorset is incarnated in Wessex, Hardy answers, with 'landscape, prehistoric antiquities, and especially old English architecture' ('General Preface' 480). Such names as 'the

Vale of Blackmoor or Blakemore', 'The Devil's Kitchen', 'Cross-in-Hand', 'Stonehenge' and 'the river Froom, or Frome' are retained *de facto* ('Preface' 480). Hardy also acknowledges the occasional deliberate intermingling of fact and imagination: 'In respect of places described under fictitious or ancient names in the novels. . . discerning people have affirmed in print that they clearly recognise the originals' ('Preface' 480). Though he alters names of places, he retains their cultural and geographical identity and in this manner walks the tightrope between fiction and fact.

To the category of altered names belong the following: Shaston ('really' Shaftesbury), Casterbridge (Dorchester), Kingsbere (Bere Regis), Wellbridge (Wool Bridge), Chalk Newton (Maiden Newton) and Flintcomb Ash (a farm near Nettecombe Tout). Hardy used them with considerable intertextual aplomb, as validated in *Tess of the d'Urbervilles*: 'On an evening in the latter part of May a middle-aged man was walking homeward from Shaston to the village of Marlott, in the adjoining vale of Blakemore or Blackmoor'(*Tess of the d'Urbervilles* 1)[12].

Hardy's geography, claims Millgate with precision, is known for its 'flexible fidelity to actuality'. Places, buildings and landmarks are modified 'in new topographical relationships, in order to meet the overriding demands of the fiction, the work of art itself' (Millgate 201). Hence, the 'texture' of Hardy's art is 'thick with remembered experience and observation, and with family and local traditions possessed so absolutely by the imagination as to be indistinguishable from memory itself' (Millgate 201). Hardy wanted to keep the regional consciousness of Dorset alive much as William Barnes, before him, had done in his poetry. Indeed, Hardy's use of the term 'Wessex' is itself intertextual in a strict sense. Before him Barnes had used it in an accurate historical sense, and later Hardy made it his own by 'extending it to the whole of south-west England east of Tamar, and in popularizing it into an everyday term' (Kay-Robinson 110).

By investing a geographical unit with cultural identity and divesting it of a nomenclatural one, Hardy indirectly asks the reader to look for indications other than names that promote recognition. Chief among place-signifiers are local custom and topographical features. The May dance in *Tess of the d'Urbervilles* and the heath in *The Return of the Native* are localised fixtures. Since the creation of Wessex entailed a conditional fictionalising of fact, the Chase as it is called in *Tess of the d'Urbervilles* is ostensibly Cranborne, a small market town south of the Blandford–Salisbury road (Pinion 274). The name changes, but not its devious topography in which Tess loses herself both literally and socially. Furthermore, in such passages as the Club-day walking and dancing at the beginning of *Tess of the d'Urbervilles*, Hardy certainly drew upon what he had seen of such events in the Vale of Blackmoor.

This is a 'semi-disguise', says Kay-Robinson rightly (111). According to her, this kind of provisional fictionalising endowed Hardy with two distinct advantages. He was 'freer to make fictional changes in a real-life scene if he gave it a fictional name' and secondly 'it was politic to disguise the setting of a story in order to avoid giving offense' (112). A similar reason for fictionalising is proffered directly by Emma Tennant, when she revises Hardy's *Tess of the d'Urbervilles*: 'I have to choose another name for our village – more a hamlet, really – where I grew up and have come back to today. . . I shall call it Nasebury. The secrecy comes not from a desire to be coy but from the need to protect the place from prying eyes. . .' (Tennant 11). 'All the other names of the places are real', such as Abbotsbury, West Bexington, Rodden, Langton Herring and Weymouth (Tennant 11).

For her *Tess*, therefore, Emma Tennant finds a ready-made intertextual device of noteworthy calibre in Wessex. It is already a consciously achieved textualisation, a transformation of a place to signifier. Since Wessex is indelibly integral to Hardy's novels, he dominates all associations with the term. Tennant builds on this assumption when she writes that Hardy's characters who 'lived' in Wessex are more real than Hardy himself. She confidently asserts that

> the flippant seductions of Alec d'Urberville linger still in all this part of Dorset; and Tess's heart-rending voice, whether uttering the low diapason of the baptism of her dying child, or singing songs with other dairymaids at Talbothays, still echoes when the winter wind whistles, when the larks sing on the high ground at Evershot. (Tennant 11)

This particular excerpt has manifold intertextual roles. In chapter three, 'The Novel' it has served to illustrate the metafictional phenomenon of an intentional confusion between illusion and reality.

Since Tennant bases her novel on connotations already established and authenticated by Hardy, she has already subscribed to intertextuality. She subsequently hones this intertextual device carefully, also making it a vehicle of metafiction. In Wessex, Hardy created an overlapping of fact and fiction without an overt metafictional intention. With Tennant it is otherwise and her intertextuality is strengthened by metafictional elements. The boundary between fact and fiction, on the obliteration of which depends Wessex, is deliberately emphasised by Tennant. Millgate records that 'literary pilgrims began to descend on Dorchester in search of Casterbridge and a tangible Wessex and in the hope of catching a glimpse of its creator, the "author of *Tess*", as he was now so often called' (Millgate 323). Tennant shrewdly and competently takes metafictional advantage of the principle underlying Millgate's observation, as will be demonstrated in the following paragraph.

While referring to Wool Manor in her novel (Tennant 162), Tennant extends a Wessex-ing process. At this juncture in her narrative, she introduces a passage from *Tess of the d'Urbervilles* verbatim, where Tess stares in fascinated horror at the portraits on the landing at Wool Manor. Tennant creates a situation in her novel where Florence Hardy peruses this passage. This intrusion underpins a metafictional proceeding, which is as follows. Wool Manor or Woolbridge House is the actual real mansion, of which Wellbridge House, where Tess and Angel spend their wedding night in *Tess of the d'Urbervilles*, is the fictional correspondent. Wellbridge, like its real counterpart, stands over the river Frome. Hardy's transformation of Wool Manor to Wellbridge paves the way for Tennant's intertextual purpose in this manner.

Tennant creates a network of alternating strands of fiction and reality in the light of the statement that Angel and his wife came to *Wool Manor* (Tennant 162, emphasis mine). Angel, a fictional figure, ought (in keeping with the principles of fiction) to have come to Wellbridge House. Instead he goes to Wool Manor, because Tennant chooses to make the two spheres of reality and illusion share a reciprocal relationship.

Anthea Zeman makes a significant remark about Wessex in the text of Beningfield's illustrated book, *Hardy Country*, that suggests how it accommodates itself to both intertextuality and metafiction. According to her, 'Hardy claimed that his landscape was the entire ancient Kingdom of Wessex – a territory that was historically of shifting shape', so that fluidity seems built into it (Beningfield 49). Hardy's Wessex was very close to the real Dorset, but he manipulated it in a geographically imprecise manner. Alterations would be made, for instance, to the location of a house, or the size of the heath.

In his repeated evocations of Wessex, Hardy was trying to assuage nostalgia and preserve the dying folk-life of a Dorset county knit by custom and place. In the process, an intertextuality of uncommon order, text and geography, developed. One question deserves to be raised at this juncture: What (if anything) would be lost, were Wessex entirely fictional? It is indeed possible to answer that intertextuality of a sophisticated kind would be lost. Hardy has shown through Wessex that the imagination does not suffer by depending on something else, which is the underlying principle of intertextuality.

NOTES

1 The subtitles of the two are 'A Romance' and 'The Sequel to Wuthering Heights' respectively. Another Victorianist novel with the same subtitle as *Possession* is Lindsay Clarke's *The Chymical Wedding: A Romance* (London: Jonathan Cape, 1989).

2 Published in 1816, Coleridge's incomplete poem is a medieval romance of the supernatural, written in what is sometimes referred to as the 'Christabel metre', that is four-foot couplets, mostly iambic and anapaestic, used with immense variety so that the line-length varies from seven, to ten or eleven syllables. Refer J. A. Cuddon, *A Dictionary of Literary Terms* (London: Penguin Books, 1979) 118.

3 This is also the design of Coleridge's poem, 'Christabel'.

4 The absence of versification does not deter the story from recalling 'Goblin Market'. Rather, it may well be Byatt's intertextual intention to imitate, but with generic alterations. There is no doubt about 'Goblin Market' being a fairy tale. A recent proof is its inclusion in Michael Patrick Hearn ed., *The Victorian Fairy Tale Book* (New York: Pantheon Books, 1988).

5 Christina Rossetti is a hidden text in another Victorianist novel as well, John Fowles's *FLW*. Nan Miller's article elucidates the comparison between Sarah and Christina painstakingly in 'Christina Rossetti and Sarah Woodruff: Two Remedies for a Divided Self', *Journal of Pre-Raphaelite Studies* (3 Nov 1982) 68–77.

6 Refer to the chapter, 'The Novel' for a similar point about revision and its retention in *FLW*.

7 The natural impulse of the journal-text is to elicit information, and in both cases, it almost succeeds in wresting the truth out of Ellen. This shall be demonstrated in the course of the chapter.

8 Emma Hardy was a real Victorian figure who kept secret diaries that came to light after her death. However, unlike Ellen Ash, she poured all her grievances against her husband Thomas Hardy, in her journal. Michael Millgate, *Thomas Hardy: A Biography* (Oxford: Oxford University Press, 1985) 324.

9 For example, at the end of chapter fifty-one, a footnote explains the phrase 'a never-say-die' as 'A black eye' (*FLW* 334). Similarly, Matthew Arnold's poem, 'To Marguerite', is acknowledged in chapter fifty-eight as a footnote (*FLW* 366).

10 Note 25 (as well as its textual counterpart) recalls with a deceptive innocence Lyell's geological discoveries about the age of the earth, which, along with Darwin's findings, were crucial in shaping the system of beliefs in Victorian society. A. S. Byatt, *Possession: A Romance* (London: Vintage, 1990) 445–46.

11 For instance, Hardy's *Tess of the d'Urbervilles* sports an epigraph from a Shakespearean play: 'Poor wounded name! my bosom, as a bed/Shall lodge thee. . . .' *The Two Gentlemen of Verona* (1.2.111–12).

12 The opening sentence from *Tess of the d'Urbervilles* is a classic instance of the complex relationship between 'real' and 'fictional' which overlap. Shaston is the ancient name of Shaftesbury; Marlott is the fictional equivalent of the 'real' place, Marnhull; while Blakemore/Blackmoor is part of the real landscape. Michael Millgate, *Thomas Hardy: A Biography* (Oxford: Oxford University Press, 1985) 324.

6 Perspectives

'In the beginning, says the Evangelist, was the Word, and the Word was with God; and the Word was God: the Logos; the great I AM, of which no predicate shall suffice. This I have believed' (Lindsay Clarke, *The Chymical Wedding* 144).

This excerpt from the foremost of texts, the Bible, indicates how its meaning is arrested at the level of the signifier, for the Word is God; there is no God beyond His Word. The clergyman in this Victorianist novel makes an intertextual execution upon an erstwhile statement of faith, turning it to one of scepticism.

What one is finally left with, then, is the text. One of the fundamental premises of intertextuality is that a text can never be completed. However, this does not necessarily imply that there are infinite possibilities of prolonging a narrative sequence. On the contrary, a well-structured novel closes certain doors as decisively as it opens others. Patrick O'Donnell remarks on the open-endedness of texts that 'a text is a fabric simultaneously being woven and unwoven' (O'Donnell x). This works ably to the advantage of the Victorianist novels, which take inspiration from Victorian texts and Victorian settings, and simultaneously exhibit a refreshing tendency to escape parental control. They refashion received notions of their parent texts[1].

The open-endedness inherent in intertextual re-writing is illustrated in the following example of Dickens's accidentally incomplete novel. *The Mystery of Edwin Drood* (hereafter referred to as *ED*) is not a Victorianist novel by any stretch of the imagination, yet its incompleteness furnishes me with an excellent sample for demonstrating intertextuality.

The Endings of *Edwin Drood*

Dickens was unwittingly responsible for intertextual endeavours by dying in the middle of writing chapter twenty-two. This has prompted many 'endings' to the novel. Normally a most meticulous writer, Dickens usually made comprehensive notes for the chapters of his novels; but none were made for the subsequent chapters of *ED*, or even for the sixth monthly part which included this chapter. While on the one hand, this has ameliorated a free play of imagination, on the other hand it has also resulted in an absence of closure. There is no 'last chapter' to exercise its tyranny upon the reader's continued speculation. This is a somewhat trying open-endedness, since no plot demands closure as insistently as a detective novel.

Various endings have been written for *ED* by various hands[2]. *The Dickens Case: the Truth about the Mystery of Edwin Drood* was written in Italian by Carlo Fruttero and Franco Lucentini and translated by Gregory Dowling. In Peter Rowland's *The Disappearance of Edwin Drood* the major characters in the story are re-visited, the mystery is examined by Sherlock Holmes, and the blatantly intertextual nature of this ending which extends its sources from Dickens to Conan Doyle is self-evident. The presence of Wilkie Collins in *The Disappearance of Edwin Drood* is engineered by advancing the suggestion that Collins murdered Dickens in Gad's Hill, because he suspected the latter of stealing his plot. This interfacing of 'life' and 'text' is very much in the style of intertextuality.

These are just a few of the twenty-five-odd novelistic and fifty-odd dramatic treatments of *ED* in the late nineteenth and early twentieth centuries. One of them, a Broadway musical called *The Mystery of Edwin Drood*, also contains a measure of self-reflexivity, since the actors poll the audience at the end to decide the murderer's identity. Besides involving the audience in structuring the narrative, this is a technique that also perpetuates the open-ended nature of Dickens's novel by ensuring a new conclusion during each performance.

The reader's own status in relation to the novel is problematic. He is placed perforce in a postmodern situation wherein the author divests himself of the responsibility of supplying an end. 'In fact, all unwillingly, one is *always* brought back to the simple distress that the book was not finished' (Angus Wilson 27, emphasis mine). *ED* is a tale half-told, pleading to be completed. Like Coleridge's 'Christabel' it teases the reader who is chained to the narrative law of 'what-happened-next'.

The attempts to find an ending for *ED* are several, and I have only referred to a few in passing to show how their intertextuality is compounded by self-reflexivity. The larger issue that these attempts point towards is that of 'returning' to a text and trying to complete it satisfactorily. From this endeavour it is but a step ahead to go back to completed texts such as *Tess of the d'Urbervilles* or *Wuthering Heights,* and rewrite them in a topically satisfying manner. This enterprise involves the identifying of sites in the plots of the *ur*-texts that are thereafter subject to a twentieth-century perspective.

Film and Intertextuality

The production of such films as *Angels and Insects* and *FLW* encourages us to consider the related question of intertextuality and cinema. The film is an'other' and different medium, with its own laws and exclusive means of juxtaposing eras or highlighting self-reflexivity. Cinematic adaptations of the Victorianist novels need to be judged on their own terms.

Like metadrama, cinema can also assert its self-consciousness by enclosing a film within a film to escape the mimetic trap of naiveté. It is thus that Karel Reisz (the director of the film *The French Lieutenant's Woman*) and Harold Pinter (who wrote the screenplay) dexterously tailor the plot of Fowles's novel while being faithful to its principle, which is exposing the artifice of its Victorian narrative. In the movie, Pinter achieves a similar deflection by enclosing the Victorian story within a modern twentieth-century one. While this Chinese-box structure casts the story of Sarah and Charles as 'only' a story, the larger, ostensibly 'real' story of the actor Mike (played by Jeremy Irons who plays the role of Charles), and the actress Anna (played by Meryl Streep who plays the role of Sarah) raises the essentially metafictional problem of the inter-relationship of life and fiction.

The film *FLW* emphasises the postmodern temper of the novel and comes remarkably close to fulfilling the narrator's dream in the novel of allowing the characters complete autonomy, because the cinematic mode phases the narrator away. The 'narrator' after all, is a novelistic device. It almost appears as though the novel requires the film to express its pressing ideology of existentialist freedom. The screenplay, however, certainly suffers from a loss of background; the magnificent Victorian preoccupations of the novel are conspicuous by their absence here. 'This, then, is Pinter's version of Fowles's narrator: a distanced perspective without a background of knowledge, 1867 without evolution and revolution, the Victorian Age without Darwin and Marx' (Knapp 58).

Since 'the two-hour film that we view contains within it a ninety-eight-minute film known, presumably, as *The French Lieutenant's Woman*' (Knapp 61), the two endings of the novel are easily transferred to the screenplay as the respective endings of the film-within-the-film and the film. The conclusions are ingeniously 'echoed' to suit the medium of the movie. The Victorian story of Sarah and Charles takes the first novelistic conclusion, and ends happily. The second and unhappy ending of the novel, where Sarah and Charles part, is brought to the story of Mike and Anna whose brief liaison during the making of the film *FLW* comes to an end.

It is significant that when Anna leaves Mike at the end of the party, a distraught Mike shouts out not her name, but that of Sarah (Conradi in '*The French Lieutenant's Woman*: novel, screenplay, film' 50). The film thereby faithfully adheres to the novel's technique of transposing fiction and reality. Mike loves Anna the actress who only plays the role of Sarah briefly: yet he calls her by the latter name, underscoring the metafictional point that the line between role-playing and real playing can become invisible. Our own fictions entrap us.

Since film is a different medium altogether, it is a moot point if the transference of a novel to celluloid is a feat of intertextuality. But within the parameters of the cinematic reproduction, there exists the metafictional principle of intertextuality as found in Fowles's text. The secret lies in discovering appropriateness, in 'the extent to which film recasts and rethinks the problems of the novel so that they will be digestible by film, which has a language, a tradition, and a logic as inescapable as fictional discourse albeit a radically different set' (Conradi in '*The French Lieutenant's Woman*: novel, screenplay, film' 49).

This takes us to a discussion of Peter Ackroyd's *The Great Fire of London* (hereafter referred to as *GFL*), not least because it unwinds the trammelled paths of producing a movie in the twentieth-century, out of a Victorian novel. Ackroyd's novel takes its title from a sentence illustrative of extreme absurdity aptly uttered by Mr F's aunt in *Little Dorrit*: ' "The Monument near London Bridge. . . was put up after the Great Fire of London; and the Great Fire of London was not the fire in which your uncle George's workshops was burned down" ' (*Little Dorrit* 159).

In *GFL*, Spenser Spender is a film-maker whose present venture is inspired by a line that persistently haunts him. The sentence is from Dickens's *Little Dorrit*: ' "I never should have touched you but I thought you were a child" ' (*Little Dorrit* 175–76, *GFL* 11, 107). Ackroyd's novel ingeniously echoes varies characters from Dickens's: Howard, a minor character, is a take-off on the garrulous Flora Finching; there is a 'little Arthur' who is an elegiac re-creation of 'little' Amy Dorrit; and Audrey whose schizophrenia is a twentieth-century version of her Victorian model Affery's paranoid fears.

Besides these superficial similarities, Ackroyd's novel also reflects the thematic obsessions of *Little Dorrit*, symbolised powerfully in the prison. For Dickens, the Marshalsea is a central metaphor. Ackroyd's novel similarly begins with a preoccupation over the Marshalsea: the characters in the narrative are all anxious to find out its location. Ackroyd shows himself as much a master of metaphor as Dickens by putting the following definition of the gaol in the mouth of his fictional character, Rowan: 'a small wound which had never healed' (*GFL* 24).

But where Ackroyd's novel unconsciously allies itself with other Victorianist ones like *Possession* and *Angels and Insects* is in selecting the séance as an integral narrative segment. For Ackroyd it becomes a means of creating metafiction. When Audrey participates in the séance she is little prepared for turning into a medium herself. This experience turns out to be a complex one, since the spirit that speaks through her claims to be 'Little Dorrit'. In the 'real' world of Ackroyd's novel, Little Dorrit is a textual fictional character, so this statement prevents the reader from suspending disbelief. In all seriousness Audrey states, ' "I am the child of the Marshalsea" ' (*GFL* 40).

While this is a deliberate fact–fiction exchange familiar to readers of metafiction, this incident simultaneously contains a deeper truth. In Little Amy Dorrit, Dickens had personified a remarkably sensitive soul in a sordid world of deceit, vanity and crime. However, there is no Little Dorrit in *GFL*, only a little Arthur who unleashes the forces of destruction. No brave, unselfish, noble little soul exists in twentieth-century London.

An intriguing intertextual question here is: which aspect of *Little Dorrit* does *GFL* find pertinent to recall? The answer is dismal: a world infested with madness, totalitarian control and emptiness. The narrative fittingly closes on an outbreak of fire. With the help of the tramps, Audrey sets fire to the film sets of 'Little Dorrit' in which Spenser Spender loses his life. Meanwhile Little Arthur short-circuits the electric connections of the prison and sets the prisoners free. As they break out pell-mell the narrator comments in Dickensian tones: 'No force on earth could have halted them, perhaps, in that moment when the system failed' (*GFL* 169). Dickens is resurrected not, after all, in a romantic union of the kind embodied in the rewarding love of Little Dorrit and Arthur Clennam, but in a violent and nihilistic act more suited to a re-working of, for instance, *A Tale of Two Cities* (1859).

Multiple Intertexts

This study of intertextuality in Victorianist fiction will be incomplete without a discussion of Lin Haire-Sergeant's novel *Heathcliff*, which is unusual among the novels looked at thus far, in that it has two famous Victorian parent texts.

The questions that *Heathcliff* provokes are many, and true to the postmodern spirit they are not laid to rest. Intertextuality in this novel takes the pattern of dialectic in the title, which underscores textuality. The title seems to be invested with a deliberate ambiguity which problematises the construct of text. On the cover page of the novel, the subtitle to *Heathcliff* is 'The Sequel to Wuthering Heights'. Inside, the subtitle is slightly changed, by being 'The Return to Wuthering Heights'. While the former is a text-conscious title containing within itself the notion of textual continuity, the latter is not a textual signifier. 'Return' is not textually marked, and neither is 'Wuthering Heights' highlighted in any way. There are no inverted commas or other indications of textualisation. This version of the subtitle alludes to Heathcliff's return to the house called Wuthering Heights. Although in the first subtitle, too, 'Wuthering Heights' is not textually underscored, the word 'sequel' is adequate to indicate the primacy of text[3].

The intertextual process continues in the encounter between Lockwood (a fictional character) and Charlotte Brontë (a real-life author), which has a further dislocating effect as Charlotte belongs naturally to the world of *Jane Eyre*. The question that arises at this juncture has to do with the inclusion of *Jane Eyre* into the narrative vacuum created by *Wuthering Heights*. Why does Haire-Sargeant take recourse to a Victorian text other than *Wuthering Heights* itself, to fill the hiatus?[4] One answer to this question is that by this means, Haire-Sargeant conveys the impression of inevitability about intertextual proceedings, where texts continually trespass into each other's territories.

Moreover, the implications of this encounter between Lockwood and Charlotte Brontë are counter to convention. Rather than the author dictating the terms of the novel, it is Lockwood who presumes to give Charlotte the facts about Heathcliff's disappearance. With this Lockwood shows himself to have come a long way from the intermediary role he plays in *Wuthering Heights*, of simply communicating Ellen Dean's intelligences to the reader.

Heathcliff takes the reality–illusion duality to its extreme possibility in the legend of the Red Lord, whose moral is 'either that the world we think we inhabit is but the dream of a sleeping giant, or, oddly, that the world around us is real but *we* are illusion' (*Heathcliff* 168), a moral that stretches metafiction to the threshold of metaphysics.

Victorianism and Rewriting

Two angles to the question of rewriting arise here. One is the role of the Victorians; the other is the way they are approached intertextually. There is an inevitability to this intertextual approach in the era of postmodernism. The Victorianist novels of this study re-present the Victorians from a point of vantage, and this vantage includes the awareness that they are texts, dealing with other texts.

What aspects of the Victorians have the Victorianists appropriated and what have they subverted? Although this question has been considered with reference to specific instances and specific novels, it is now time to see where these individual threads lead. This also raises the related question of what comprises the 'Victorian' as a recognisable entity.

With novels like *Tess*, *WSS* and *Heathcliff*, the Victorian component is readily available in the form of plots of Victorian novels by Hardy,

Charlotte Brontë and Charlotte and Emily Brontë respectively. The inter-referencing between these novels is very straightforward, with the element of metafiction redeeming the latter novels from being 'mere' sequels.

But there are other, more general characteristics that contribute to the outline of the Victorian period for us. The Victorian period was historically the era when gender consciousness came to be debated in England, and women's voices came to be heard, in many public spheres. This is a socio-historical fact that any novelist dealing with the Victorian period must take into the reckoning. One common concern of all these Victorianist novels is the issue of gender. Victorianist novels consider this factor from various perspectives; for example, *Possession* deals with the problems and frustrations of being a woman writer in the Victorian period by presenting individual characters like Christabel and Ellen. It also engages with the more public female space of the séance, which came to be associated with women in the Victorian period.

To a certain extent, Victorianist novels are like historical novels in their attempt to evoke the ambience of a certain era. But having evoked it, they 'do things' with the era primarily towards a self-reflexive end. Gender-debate becomes a Victorian landmark that these novels recognise and trust their readers to recognise as well.

An obvious lead at this juncture – given the postmodernist tendency for 'play' – is the possibility that the Victorianists may take an obvious historical counter and alter it through parody. *Possession* does this in the character of Leonora Stern. This would be a classic instance of the divergence of paths between a Victorianist novel and a historical novel set in the Victorian period. The latter kind would never consider the implications of stretching a particular historical element to touch the limits of absurdity or to provoke laughter.

Besides individual plots and era-defining issues like the woman question, the Victorianist novels also rely on literary tradition for optimal relevance. In the creation of a quintessential and famous Victorian poet, for example, Byatt relies on the dramatic monologue. Her fictional poet, Randolph Ash, recalls Browning primarily because he is a writer of dramatic monologues, and has written a monologue called 'Mummy Possest' which is remarkably similar to Browning's 'Mr Sludge, "the Medium" ', also a dramatic monologue.

Here then is a case where we have a particular literary genre standing as a trope for the Victorians. The Victorianist novelist's ability to use this trope successfully reflects on the way in which particular historical periods are shaped in the public, here a specifically academic mind. The student of literature knows the Victorian period to be that of the dramatic monologue. If he were to find in a period novel the portrait of a famous writer of dramatic monologues, it would be natural for him to locate the period as Victorian.

What constitutes the Victorian, then, varies from novel to novel. But all the novels depend on certain received notions of the definition of the Victorian period, a period in which certain social or literary norms prevailed over others.

We can go on to examine the role of stereotypes and the popular imagination in order to develop the argument about Victorian'ness' more thoroughly. But this has not been possible in this study as we have focussed on genre and its functioning in intertextuality. However, a study of the way in which stereotypes are planted and exploited by writers and readers of texts would be an important milestone in carving the full measure of intertextuality. A novel like *FLW*, would be better highlighted in such a study, for instance. Similar studies on other kinds of period-inspired intertextuality are other possibilities.

Concluding Statements

Our first aim in this book, as stated in the introduction, was to catalogue the various types of intertextuality. This has demonstrated the versatility of the generic principle in producing intertextuality. The fundamental definition of intertextuality as a self-reflexive procedure preoccupied with the centuries-old problem of representation, has emerged systematically in the generic analyses of Victorianist novels. Devices like the epigraph and the footnote aid admirably in this direction. Frow enforces this observation with his declaration that intertextual structures are represented in a variety of forms. These include 'cultural and ideological norms', 'the conventions of genre', 'connotations and collocative sets', 'clichés, formulae, or proverbs' and 'other texts' (Frow 45).

Bakhtin's dialogic theory has been of enormous assistance in establishing intertextuality as a natural property of the novel. The chapters on genre illustrate this truth variously but incontrovertibly, and the Victorianist novels acquit themselves creditably by displaying their embedding capabilities.

In considering 'Why the Victorians?' in the introduction we have already discussed the last objective of this study. The objective of studying the relationship between mimetic and intertextual theories of art does not lend itself to an unequivocal answer, and can, at best, only be discussed. Chapters one to three, especially, study the ways in which representative procedures are deliberately foregrounded, cautioning the reader against losing himself in the narrative. Plato's objection to literature was made on the grounds that it is twice-removed from the truth, since it persuaded the reader to accept a world of illusion as real. Intertextuality, being less a representation of the real world than a reassessment of prior texts, operates to create an awareness in the reader of the artefact of literature; to this extent it is opposed in intention to the Platonic and Aristotelian theories of mimesis.

Intertextuality denies autonomy to individual literary productions by interjecting cross-referencing procedures at the stage of inception and beyond. These prompt an alert reader to look outside the margins of the text and acknowledge it as a representation. This knowledge helps him to escape the seductive charm of the imaginary world of literature, which Plato defined as iniquitous to human intellect and well-being. Under these circumstances, intertextuality is a safeguard against an inherent 'danger' expressed by the mimetic theory of art.

In the ongoing evolution of literary tradition, each writer believes that a predecessor text contains a space that requires to be filled. He also believes that he is equipped to fill it. Intertextual activities impress upon the literary lineage the image of a palimpsest, with each successive author competing to impose his writing on a previous textual perspective. Thus, by being reinscribed, the death of the author is forever forestalled[5].

NOTES

1 Baxandall's catalogue enumerates the kind of intriguing transformations that are capable of being effected by self-conscious re-writings : 'draw on', 'resort to', 'avail oneself of', 'appropriate from', 'misunderstand', 'reconstitute', 'engage with', 'differentiate oneself from', 'quote', 'align oneself with', 'copy', 'emulate', 'travesty', 'parody', 'subvert' and 'perpetuate', are among these. Quoted in Clayton and Rothstein, eds. *Influence and Intertextuality in Literary History* (Wisconsin: Wisconsin University Press, 1991) 6–7.

2 The source of this information is list Victoria which discussed the various endings to *ED* in October 1995.

3 A commercial angle is also identifiable in the use of 'Sequel'. That publishing constraints operated to change 'Return' to 'Sequel' is not an implausible speculation.

4 Haire-Sargeant's ingenious answer to the question of Heathcliff's parentage comes from *Jane Eyre*, as she identifies Rochester and Bertha as Heathcliff's father and mother respectively.

5 This declaration contests Roland Barthes's confident assertion of the death of the author: 'We know that to give writing its future, it is necessary to overthrow the myth : the birth of the reader must be at the cost of the death of the author'. Roland Barthes, 'The death of the author', *Modern Criticism and Theory: A Reader,* ed. David Lodge (London and New York: Longman, 1988) 171–72.

★ ★ ★

Bibliography

PRIMARY SOURCES

Victorianist

Books

Ackroyd, Peter. *The Great Fire of London*. 1982. London: Penguin Books, 1993.

Byatt, A. S. *Angels and Insects*. 1992. London: Vintage, 1993.

———. *Possession: A Romance*. 1990. London: Vintage, 1991.

Clarke, Lindsay. *The Chymical Wedding: A Romance*. London: Jonathan Cape, 1989.

Fowles, John. *The French Lieutenant's Woman*. 1969. London: Pan Books, 1987.

Haire-Sargeant, Lin. *Heathcliff: The Sequel to Wuthering Heights*. 1992. Arrow Books, 1993.

Lodge, David. *Nice Work*. 1988. London: Penguin, 1989.

Rhys, Jean. *Wide Sargasso Sea*. 1966. Harmondsworth: Penguin Books, 1983.

Swift, Graham. *Ever After*. London: Picador, 1992.

Tennant, Emma. *Tess*. London: Harper Collins Publishers, 1993.

Victorian

Poetry

Browning, Robert. *Robert Browning's Poems and Plays: The Ring and the Book, 1868–69*. Vol. 3. Everyman's Library. London: Dent, 1962.

———. 'Mr Sludge, "The Medium"'. *Dramatis Personae*. Ed. F. B. Pinion. London: Collins Publishers, 1969. 113–60.

Dickinson, Emily. *The Complete Poems of Emily Dickinson*. Ed. Thomas H. Johnson. 1890. Delhi: Kalyani Publishers, 1960.

Donne, John. 'Loves Alchymie'. *The Complete English Poems*. Ed. David Campbell. Everyman's Library, 1985. 86–87.

Rossetti, Christina. 'Goblin Market'. *A Choice of Christina Rossetti's Verse*. London: Faber and Faber, 1970. 13–28.

Shatto, Susan. Ed. *Tennyson's 'Maud': A definitive edition*. London: The Athlone Press, 1986.

Thwaite, Anthony. *Victorian Voices*. Oxford: Oxford University Press, 1980.

NOVELS

Brontë, Charlotte. *Jane Eyre*. 1847. London: The Zodiac Press, 1981.

Brontë, Emily. *Wuthering Heights: with Selected Poems*. 1847. Ed. Philip Henderson. Dent: London, Melbourne and Toronto. Everyman's Library, 1978.

Dickens, Charles. *Great Expectations*. 1860–61. Ed. Angus Calder. Harmondsworth: Penguin, 1965.

———. *Little Dorrit*. 1857. London: Penguin Books, 1994.

———. *The Mystery of Edwin Drood*. 1870. London: Penguin Books, 1993.

Hardy, Thomas. 'General Preface to the Wessex Edition of 1912'. *Far from the Madding Crowd*. 1874. Delhi: Oxford University Press, 1984. 477–83.

———. *A Pair of Blue Eyes*. 1873. Delhi: Surjeet Publications, 1988.

———. *Tess of the d'Urbervilles*. 1891. New York: Bantam Books, 1981.

Hawthorne, Nathaniel. *The House of the Seven Gables*. 1851. New Delhi: Eurasia Publishing House, n.d.

SECONDARY SOURCES

BOOKS

Abrams, M. H. *Doing Things with Texts: Essays in Criticism and Critical Theory*. Ed. Michael Fischer. New York: W. W. Norton and Co., 1989.

Ackroyd, Peter. *Dickens*. London: Sinclair–Stevenson, 1990.

Angier, Carole. *Jean Rhys: Life and Work*. London: Andre Deutsch, 1990.

Aristotle. 'On the Art of Poetry'. *Classical Literary Criticism*. Trans. T. S. Dorsch. London: Penguin Books, 1965. 29–75.

Armstrong, Isobel. *Victorian Poetry: Poetry, Poetics and Politics*. London and New York: Routledge, 1993.

Arnold, Mathew. 'The Study of Poetry'. 1880. *English Critical Texts: 16th Century to 20th Century*. Eds. D. J. Enright and Ernst de Chickera. 1962. Delhi: Oxford University Press, 1987. 260–85.

Bakhtin, M. M. *The Dialogic Imagination: Four Essays*. Ed. Michael Holquist. Trans. Caryl Emerson and Michael Holquist. Austin: University of Texas Press, 1981.

Bakhtin, M. M. and **P. N. Medvedev.** *The Formal Method in Literary Scholarship: A Critical Introduction to Sociological Poetics*. Trans. Albert J. Wehrle. Cambridge, Mass.: Harvard University Press, 1985.

Bakhtin, Mikhail and **V. N. Volosinov.** 'Discourse in Life and Discourse in Art (Concerning Sociological Poetics)'. *Contemporary Literary Criticism: Literary and Cultural Studies*. Eds. Robert Con Davis and Ronald Schleifer. New York and London: Longman, 1989. 392–410.

Baldick, Chris. *The Concise Oxford Dictionary of Literary Terms*. Oxford: Oxford University Press, 1990.

Barth, John. *The Friday Book: Essays and Other Nonfiction*. New York: G. P. Putnam's Sons, 1984.

Barthes, Roland. 'The death of the author'. *Modern Criticism and Theory: A Reader*. Ed. David Lodge. London and New York: Longman, 1988. 167–72.

——. 'From Work to Text'. *Textual Strategies: Perspectives in Post-Structuralist Criticism*. Ed. Josué V. Harari. 1979. London: Methuen, 1980. 73–81.

Basham, Diana. *The Trial of Woman: Feminism and the Occult Sciences in Victorian Literature and Society*. New York: New York University Press, 1992.

Battiscombe, Georgina. *Christina Rossetti: A Divided Life*. London: Constable, 1981.

Beer, Gillian. 'Origins and Oblivion in Victorian Narrative'. *Arguing with the Past: Essays in Narrative from Woolf to Sidney*. London and New York: Routledge, 1989. 12–33.

——. *The Romance*. The Critical Idiom Series. Ed. John D. Jump. London: Methuen and Co., 1970.

Beer, Patricia. *Reader, I Married Him: A Study of the Women Characters of Jane Austen, Charlotte Bronte, Elizabeth Gaskell and George Eliot*. London: The Macmillan Press Ltd., 1974.

Beningfield, Gordon. Introduction. *Hardy Country*. London: Allen Lane (Penguin Books Ltd.), 1983.

Blank, G. Kim, and **Margot K. Louis.** Eds. *Influence and Resistance in Nineteenth-Century English Poetry*. London: Macmillan, 1993.

Bloom, Harold. *The Anxiety of Influence: A Theory of Poetry*. New York: Oxford University Press, 1973.

Bold, Alan. *The Ballad*. The Critical Idiom Series. Ed. John D. Jump. London: Methuen, 1971.

Booth, Wayne C. *The Rhetoric of Fiction*. 1961. Chicago: University of Chicago Press, 1968.

Borges, Jorge Luis. *Labyrinths: Selected Stories and Other Writings*. Ed. Donald A. Yates and James E. Irby. 1962. Harmondsworth: Penguin, 1970.

Bradbury, Malcolm, Ed. *The Novel Today: Contemporary Writers on Modern Fiction*. Glasgow: Fontana, 1977.

———. 'The Novelist as Impresario: John Fowles and His Magus'. *Possibilities: Essays on the State of the Novel*. London: Oxford University Press, 1973. 256–71.

Brooke-Rose, Christine. *Stories, theories and things*. Cambridge: Cambridge University Press, 1991.

Buckley, Jerome Hamilton. 'The Revolt From Reason'. *The Victorian Temper: A Study in Literary Culture.* 1951. Cambridge, Mass: Harvard University Press, 1978. 185–206.

Burrow, J. A. *Medieval Writers and their Work: Middle English Literature and its Background 1100–1500*. Oxford: Oxford University Press, 1982.

Byatt, A. S. *Passions of the Mind: Selected Writings*. New York: Turtle Bay Books, 1992.

Cassis, A. F. *The Twentieth Century English Novel: An Annotated Bibliography of General Criticism*. New York: Garland Publishing Inc., 1977.

Cave, Terence. *Recognitions: A Study in Poetics*. Oxford: Clarendon Press, 1988.

Clayton, Jay, and **Eric Rothstein.** Eds. *Influence and Intertextuality in Literary History*. Wisconsin: University of Wisconsin Press, 1991.

Coleridge, Samuel Taylor. *'Biographia Literaria:* Chapter XIV'. 1817. *English Critical Texts: 16th Century to 20th Century*. Eds. D. J. Enright and Ernst de Chickera. Delhi: Oxford University Press, 1987. 190–97.

Conradi, Peter. *John Fowles*. London: Methuen, 1982.

Cuddon, J. A. *A Dictionary of Literary Terms*. Rev. ed. London: Penguin, 1982.

Culler, Jonathan. *Structuralist Poetics: Structuralism, Linguistics and the Study of Literature.* London: Routledge and Kegan Paul, 1975.

Darwin, Charles. *The Origin of Species*. 1859. London: Dent, 1971.

Davidson, Arnold E. *Jean Rhys*. New York: Frederick Ungar Publishing Co., 1985.

Dubrow, Heather. *Genre*. The Critical Idiom Series. Ed. John D. Jump. London: Methuen, 1982.

Eco, Umberto. 'Casablanca: Cult Movies and Intertextual Collage'. *Modern Criticism and Theory: A Reader*. Ed. David Lodge. 1988. London and New York: Longman, 1991. 446–55.

Eco, Umberto, et al. *Interpretation and Overinterpretation*. Ed. Stefan Collini. New York: Cambridge University Press, 1992.

Eco, Umberto. *The Role of the Reader: Explorations in the Semiotics of Texts*. Bloomington: Indiana University Press, 1979.

Forbes, Patricia, and **Muriel Holland Smith.** Eds. *Harrap's Compact Dictionnaire: Anglais–Francais/Francais–Anglais*. Rev. ed. Helen Knox. London and Paris: Harrap, 1984.

Ford, Boris. Ed. *From Dickens to Hardy*. Vol. 6 of The Pelican Guide to English Literature. Penguin Books, 1958.

Forster, E. M. *Aspects of the Novel*. 1927. Ed. Oliver Stallybrass. Harmondsworth: Penguin, 1974.

Forsyte, Charles. *The Decoding of Edwin Drood*. London: Victor Gollancz Ltd., 1980.

Fowles, John. *The Aristos*. 1964. Rev. ed. London: Jonathan Cape, 1980.

——. 'Hardy and the Hag'. *Thomas Hardy After Fifty Years*. Ed. Lance St John Butler. London: Macmillan, 1977. 28–42.

Frow, John. 'Intertextuality and Ontology'. *Intertextuality: Theories and Practices*. Eds. Michael Worton and Judith Still. Manchester: Manchester University Press, 1990. 45–55.

Frye, Northrop. *Anatomy of Criticism: Four Essays*. 1957. Princeton: Princeton University Press, 1971.

Garlick, Barbara. 'Christina Rossetti and the Gender Politics of Fantasy'. *The Victorian Fantasists: Essays on Culture, Society and Belief in the Mythopoeic Fiction of the Victorian Age*. Ed. Kath Filmer. London: Macmillan, 1991. 133–52.

Genette, Gerard. *Narrative Discourse*. 1972. Trans. Jane E. Lewin. Oxford: Basil Blackwell, 1980.

Gilbert, Sandra M., and **Susan Gubar.** *The Madwoman in the Attic: The Woman Writer and the Nineteenth-Century Literary Imagination*. New Haven: Yale University Press, 1979.

Greenblatt, Stephen, and **Giles Gunn.** Introduction. *Redrawing the Boundaries: The Transformation of English and American Literary Studies*. Eds. Stephen Greenblatt and Giles Gunn. New York: The Modern Language Association of America, 1992. 1–11.

Greene, Gayle, and **Coppelia Kahn.** Eds. *Making A Difference: Feminist Literary Criticism*. London: Routledge, 1985.

Halperin, John. Ed. *The Theory of the Novel: New Essays*. New York: Oxford University Press, 1974.

Hawthorn, Jeremy. *A Glossary of Contemporary Literary Theory*. Second Ed. London: Edward Arnold, 1994.

Henderson, Lesley. Ed. *Contemporary Novelists*. 5th Ed. Chicago and London: St James Press, 1991.

Herdman, John. *The Double in Nineteenth-Century Fiction*. Hampshire: The Macmillan Press Ltd., 1990.

Holquist, Michael. Introduction. M. M. Bakhtin. *The Dialogic Imagination: Four Essays*. Trans. Caryl Emerson and Michael Holquist. Austin : University of Texas Press, 1981. xv–xxxiv.

Hutcheon, Linda. *Narcissistic Narrative: The Metafictional Paradox*. 1980. London and New York: Methuen, 1984.

James, Louis. *Jean Rhys*. 'Critical Studies of Caribbean Writers'. Gen. Ed. Mervyn Morris. London: Longman, 1978.

Jehlen, Myra. 'Gender'. *Critical Terms for Literary Study*. Eds. Frank Lentricchia and Thomas McLaughlin. Chicago: Chicago University Press, 1990. 263–73.

Kay-Robinson, Denys. 'Hardy's Wessex'. *The Genius of Thomas Hardy*. Ed. Margaret Drabble. London: Weidenfeld and Nicolson, 1976. 110–18.

Klingopulos, G. D. 'The Literary Scene'. *From Dickens to Hardy*. Vol. 6 of The Pelican Guide to English Literature. Penguin Books, 1958. 59–116.

Kristeva, Julia. *Desire in Language: A Semiotic Approach to Literature and Art*. Ed. Leon S. Roudiez. Trans. Thomas Gora et al. Columbia: Columbia University Press, 1980.

Kundera, Milan. *The Art of the Novel*. Trans. Linda Asher. London: Faber and Faber Ltd., 1988.

Langbaum, Robert. *The Poetry of Experience: The Dramatic Monologue in Modern Literary Tradition*. Chicago: University of Chicago Press, 1985.

Leavis, F. R., and **Q. D. Leavis.** *Dickens the Novelist*. London: Chatto and Windus, 1970.

Levine, George. 'Victorian Studies'. *Redrawing the Boundaries: The Transformation of English and American Studies*. Ed. Greenblatt and Gunn. Modern Language Association, 1992. 130–53.

Lodge, David. *After Bakhtin: Essays on Fiction and Criticism*. London and New York: Routledge, 1990.

———. *The Art of Fiction: Illustrated from Classic and Modern Texts*. London: Secker and Warburg, 1992.

———. *The Novelist at the Crossroads: and other essays on fiction and criticism*. 1971. London: Ark Paperbacks, 1986.

Loveday, Simon. *The Romance of John Fowles*. New York: St Martin's Press, 1985.

Lukács, Georg. *The Historical Novel*. 1937. Trans. Hannah and Stanley Mitchell. Boston: Beacon Press, 1963.

McHale, Brian. *Postmodernist Fiction*. New York: Methuen, 1987.

McKnight, Natalie. '*Little Dorrit's* Misfits: Between the Sun and the Cell'. *Idiots, Madmen and Other Prisoners in Dickens*. New York: St Martin's Press, 1993. 111–28.

Millgate, Michael. *Thomas Hardy: A Biography*. 1982. Oxford: Oxford University Press, 1985.

Mitchell, W. J. T. 'Representation'. *Critical Terms for Literary Study*. Eds. Frank Lentricchia and Thomas McLaughlin. Chicago: Chicago University Press, 1990. 11–22.

Moi, Toril. Ed. *The Kristeva Reader*. New York: Columbia University Press, 1986.

Morgan, Rosemarie. *Women and Sexuality in the Novels of Thomas Hardy*. 1988. London and New York: Routledge, 1991.

Nair, Rukmini Bhaya. 'Gender, genre, and generative grammar: Deconstructing the matrimonial column'. *Language, Text and Context: Essays in Stylistics*. Ed. Michael Toolan. London and New York: Routledge, 1992. 227–54.

———. 'The Pedigree of the White Stallion: Postcoloniality and Literary History'. *The Uses of Literary History*. Ed. Marshall Brown. Durham: Duke University Press, 1995.

O'Donnell, Patrick, and **Robert Con Davis.** Eds. *Intertextuality and Contemporary American Fiction*. Baltimore and London: John Hopkins University Press, 1989.

Ortega y Gasset, Jose. *The Dehumanization of Art: and other Essays on Art, Culture and Literature*. 1948. Princeton: Princeton University Press, 1968.

Peer, Willie van. Ed. *The Taming of the Text: Explorations in Language, Literature and Culture.* 1989. London and New York: Routledge, 1991.

Pinion, F. B. *A Tennyson Companion: Life and Works*. London: Macmillan, 1984.

———. *A Hardy Companion: A Guide to the Works of Thomas Hardy and their Background*. 1968. London: The Macmillan Press Ltd., 1984.

Plato. *Republic*. Trans. Robin Waterfield. Oxford: Oxford University Press, 1994.

Pollard, Arthur. Ed. *The Victorians.* Volume 6 of the Penguin History of Literature. 1969. London: Penguin Books, 1993.

Radford, Jean. Ed. *The Progress of Romance: The Politics of Popular Fiction*. London: Routledge and Kegan Paul, 1986.

Rhys, Jean. *Smile Please: An Unfinished Autobiography*. London: Penguin, 1979.

Riffaterre, Michael. *Text Production*. Trans. Terese Lyons. New York: Columbia University Press, 1983.

Rose, Margaret A. *Parody: Ancient, Modern, and Post-Modern*. Cambridge: Cambridge University Press, 1993.

Rowe, John Carlos. 'Postmodernist Studies'. *Redrawing the Boundaries: The Transformation of English and American Studies*. New York: Modern Language Association, 1992.

Said, Edward W. *Orientalism*. New York: Vintage, 1978.

———. 'The Text, the World, the Critic'. *Textual Strategies: Perspectives in Post-Structuralist Criticism*. Ed. Josué V. Harari. Cornell University Press, 1979. 161–88.

Schmidt, A. V. C., and **Nicolas Jacobs.** Eds. *Medieval English Romances: Part Two*. London: Hodder and Stoughton, 1980.

Scholes et al. *Text Book: An Introduction to Literary Language*. New York: St Martin's Press, 1988.

Scott, A. F. *Current Literary Terms: A Concise Dictionary of their Origin and Use*. London: Macmillan, 1965.

Seymour-Smith, Martin. *Hardy*. London: Bloomsbury, 1994.

Shaw, Harry. *Dictionary of Literary Terms*. New York: McGraw-Hill Book Co. 1972.

Showalter, Elaine. *A Literature of Their Own: British Women Novelists from Brontë to Lessing*. 1977. Princeton: Princeton University Press, 1982.

———. Ed. *Speaking of Gender*. New York and London: Routledge, 1989.

Sidney, Philip. 'An Apology for Poetry'. 1595. *English Critical Texts: 16th Century to 20th Century*. Eds. D. J. Enright and Ernst de Chickera. 1962. Delhi: Oxford University Press, 1987. 3–49.

Silvermann, Hugh J. *Textualities: Between Hermeneutics and Deconstruction*. New York and London: Routledge, 1994.

Sinfield, Alan. *The Dramatic Monologue*. The Critical Idiom Series. Ed. John D. Jump. London: Methuen and Co., 1977.

Sperber, Dan, and **Deirdre Wilson.** *Relevance: Communication and Cognition*. Oxford: Basil Blackwell, 1986.

Staley, Thomas F. *Jean Rhys: A Critical Study*. London: Macmillan, 1979.

Thomas, Frances. *Christina Rossetti: A Biography*. 1992. London: Virago Press, 1994.

Tillotson, Kathleen. *Novels of the Eighteen-Forties*. 1954. Oxford: Clarendon Press, 1985.

Todorov, Tzvetan. 'Literary Genres'. *Twentieth Century Literary Theory: An Introductory Anthology*. Eds. Vassilis Lambropoulos and David Neal Miller. State University of New York Press, 1987. 191–204.

Williams, D. A. *The Monster in the Mirror: Studies in Nineteenth Century Realism*. Oxford: Oxford University Press, 1978.

Worton, Michael, and **Judith Still.** Introduction. *Intertextuality: Theories and Practices*. Eds. Michael Worton and Judith Still. Manchester: Manchester University Press, 1990. 1–44.

Wilson, Angus. Introduction. *The Mystery of Edwin Drood*. Ed. Arthur J. Cox. London: Penguin Books, 1993. 11–28.

Wyndham, Francis. Introduction. *Wide Sargasso Sea*. 1966. Harmondsworth: Penguin, 1968. 5–11.

Young, G. M. *Portrait of an Age: Victorian England*. London: Oxford University Press, 1977.

Zeman, Anthea. The Text in Gordon Beningfield. *Hardy Country*. London: Allen Lane (Penguin Books Ltd.), 1983.

Journal Articles

Bialostoksy, D. H. 'Booth's Rhetoric, Bakhtin's Dialogics and the Future of Novel Criticism'. *Novel* 18 (Spring 1985): 223–26.

Bloom, Harold. 'How to Read a Poem: Browning's *Childe Roland*'. *Georgia Review* 28 (Fall 1974): 404–18.

——. 'The Necessity of Misreading'. *Georgia Review* 29 (Summer 1975): 267–88.

Booker, M. Keith. 'What We Have Instead of God: Sexuality, Textuality and Infinity in *The French Lieutenant's Woman*'. *Novel* 24.2 (Winter 1991): 178–98.

Bowen, Deborah. 'The Riddler Riddled: Reading the Epigraphs in John Fowles' *The French Lieutenant's Woman*'. *The Journal of Narrative Technique* 25 (Winter 1995): 67–90.

Brown, Ruth Christiani. '*The French Lieutenant's Woman* and *Pierre*: Echo and Answer'. *Modern Fiction Studies* 31.1 (Spring 1985): 115–31.

Bump, Jerome. 'The Narrator as Protoreader in *The French Lieutenant's Woman*'. *Victorian Newsletter* 74 (Fall 1988): 16–18.

Byatt, A. S. 'A hundred years after: twelve writers reflect on Tennyson's achievement and influence'. *Times Literary Supplement* 8 Feb 1992.

Campbell, Elizabeth. 'Of Mothers and Merchants: Female Economics in Christina Rossetti's "Goblin Market" '. *Victorian Studies* 33.3 (Spring 1990): 393–410.

Conradi, Peter J. '*The French Lieutenant's Woman*: novel, screenplay, film'. *Critical Quarterly* 24.1 (Spring 1982): 41–57.

Culler, Jonathan. 'Literary History, Allegory, and Semiology'. *New Literary History* 7 (Winter 1976): 259–70.

DeVitis, A. A., and **William J. Palmer.** '*A Pair of Blue Eyes* flash at *The French Lieutenant's Woman*'. *Contemporary Literature* 15.1 (Winter 1974): 90–101.

Dorst, John D. 'Neck-riddle as a Dialogue of Genres: "Applying Bakhtin's Genre Theory" '. *Journal of American Folklore*. 96. 382 (Oct–Dec 1983): 413–33.

Eddins, Dwight. 'John Fowles: Existence as Authorship'. *Contemporary Literature* 17.2 (Spring 1976): 204–22.

Fish, Thomas E. 'Browning and Mr Sludge: The Vista and the Impasse of Character'. *Studies in Browning and his Circle* 11.2 (Fall 1983): 61–76.

Flaherty, Peter. 'Reading Carnival: Towards a Semiotics of History'. *Clio* 15.4 (Summer 1986): 411–28.

Harrison, Anthony. 'Matthew Arnold's Gipsies: Intertextuality and the New Historicism'. *Victorian Poetry* 29.4 (Winter 1991): 365–83.

Hayman, D. 'Toward a Mechanics of Mode: Beyond Bakhtin'. *Novel* 16.2 (Winter 1983): 101–20.

Holmes, Frederick M. 'History, Fiction, and the Dialogic Imagination: John Fowles's *A Maggot*'. *Contemporary Literature* 32.2 (Summer 1991): 229–43.

Holt, Terrence. ' "Men Sell Not Such in Any Town": Exchange in Goblin Market'. *Victorian Poetry* 28.1 (Spring 1990): 51–67.

Johnson A. J. B. 'Realism in *The French Lieutenant's Woman*'. *Journal of Modern Literature* 8.2 (1980/81): 287–302.

Jones, Grace. 'Literary Kinship: Nathaniel Hawthorne, John Fowles, and their Scarlet Women'. *The South Atlantic Quarterly* 86.1 (Winter 1987): 69–78.

Kincaid, James R. 'Antithetical Criticism, Harold Bloom, and Victorian Poetry'. Review. *Victorian Poetry* 14 (Winter 1976): 365–82.

Knapp, Shoshana. 'The Transformation of a Pinter Screenplay: Freedom and Calculators in *The French Lieutenant's Woman*'. *Modern Drama* 28.1 (Mar 1985): 55–70.

Lewis, Janet E., and **Barry N. Olshen.** 'John Fowles and the Medieval Romance Tradition'. *Modern Fiction Studies* 31.1 (Spring 1985): 15–30.

Man, Glenn K. S. 'The Intertextual Discourses of *The French Lieutenant's Woman*'. *New Orleans Review* 15.2 (Summer 1988): 54–61.

Mansfield, Elizabeth. 'A Sequence of Endings: The Manuscripts of *The French Lieutenant's Woman*'. *Journal of Modern Literature*. 8.2 (1980–81): 275–86.

McDaniel, Ellen. 'Games and Godgames in *The Magus* and *The French Lieutenant's Woman*'. *Modern Fiction Studies* 31.1(Spring 1985): 31–42.

Miller, Nan. 'Christina Rossetti and Sarah Woodruff: Two Remedies for a Divided Self'. *The Journal of Pre-Raphaelite Studies* 3 (Nov 1982): 68–77.

Morson, G. S. 'Bakhtin, Genres, and Temporality'. *New Literary History*. 22 (Autumn 1991): 1071–92.

Nair, Rukmini Bhaya, et al. 'Lines of Metaphoricity, and Creative Metaphors as Situated Risk-Taking'. *Journal of Literary Semantics* 17.1 (1988): 20–40.

Oates, Joyce Carol. 'Romance and Anti-Romance: from Bronte's *Jane Eyre* to Rhys's *Wide Sargasso Sea*'. *The Virginia Quarterly Review* 61.1 (Winter 1985): 44–58.

Patterson, David. 'Mikhail Bakhtin and the Dialogical Dimensions of the Novel'. *Journal of Aesthetics and Art Criticism* 44.2 (Winter 1985): 131–9.

Pearce, Richard. 'The Present and Future States of Novel Criticism: Our Two-Headed Profession'. *Novel* 18.3 (Spring 1985): 223–26.

Porter, Dennis. 'Of Heroines and Victims: Jean Rhys and *Jane Eyre*'. *The Massachusetts Review* 17 (Autumn 1976): 540–52.

Riffaterre, Michael. 'Intertextual Representation: on Mimesis as Interpretive Discourse'. *Critical Inquiry* 11 (Spring 1984): 141–62.

——. 'The Intertextual Unconscious'. *Critical Inquiry* 13.2 (Winter 1987): 371–85.

——. 'The Mind's Eye: Memory and Textuality'. *Romanic Review* 79 (Jan 1988): 7–21.

——. 'On Narrative Subtexts: Proust's Magic Lantern'. *Style* 22.3 (Fall 1988): 450–66.

Scruggs, Charles. 'The Two Endings of *The French Lieutenant's Woman*'. *Modern Fiction Studies* 31 (Spring 1985): 95–113.

Smith, Frederik N. 'The Endings of *The French Lieutenant's Woman*: Another Speculation on the Manuscript'. *Journal of Modern Literature* 14 (Spring 1988): 579–84.

——. 'Revision and the Style of Revision in *The French Lieutenant's Woman*'. *Modern Fiction Studies* 31.1 (Spring 1985): 85–94.

Thorpe, Michael. ' "The Other Side": *Wide Sargasso Sea* and *Jane Eyre*'. *Ariel* 8.3 (July 1976): 99–110.

Weeks, Jeffrey. 'The Late-Victorian Stew of Sexualities'. *Victorian Studies* 35 (Summer 1992): 409–15.

Yelin, Louise. 'Cultural Cartography: A. S. Byatt's *Possession* and the Politics of Victorian Studies'. *Victorian Newsletter* 81 (Spring 1992): 38–41.

Electronic Mail

Burnette, Michaelyn. 'Drood'. E-mail to Nalini Iyer. 10 October 1995.

Clark, Denise. 'Re: Edwin Drood'. E-mail to multiple recipients of list Victoria. 10 October 1995.

Martin, Carol. 'Edwin Drood – Reply'. E-mail to multiple recipients of list Victoria. 10 October 1995.

Morgan, William W. 'Re: Tess' Rape'. E-mail to multiple recipients of list Victoria. 8 April 1996.

Nemesvari, Richard. 'Tess' Rape'. E-mail to multiple recipients of list Victoria. 5 April 1996.

Prasch, Thomas. 'A Dissent on "Angels and Insects" '. E-mail to multiple recipients of list Victoria. 29 February 1996.

Wilson, Keith. 'Re: Tess' Rape'. E-mail to multiple recipients of list Victoria. 5 April 1996.

***

Index